Situational Leadershi
Complete Self-Asses:

MW00721307

The guidance in this Self-A   p
best practices and standar᷿᷿ᴗ ...
and quality management. The guidance is also based on the professional
judgment of the individual collaborators listed in the Acknowledgments.

Notice of rights

Trademarks

Table of Contents

About The Art of Service

The Art of Service, Business Process Architects since 2000, is dedicated to helping stakeholders achieve excellence.

Defining, designing, creating, and implementing a process to solve a stakeholders challenge or meet an objective is the most valuable role… In EVERY group, company, organization and department.

Unless you're talking a one-time, single-use project, there should be a process. Whether that process is managed and implemented by humans, AI, or a combination of the two, it needs to be designed by someone with a complex enough perspective to ask the right questions.

Someone capable of asking the right questions and step back and say, 'What are we really trying to accomplish here? And is there a different way to look at it?'

With The Art of Service's Standard Requirements Self-Assessments, we empower people who can do just that — whether their title is marketer, entrepreneur, manager, salesperson, consultant, Business Process Manager, executive assistant, IT Manager, CIO etc... —they are the people who rule the future. They are people who watch the process as it happens, and ask the right questions to make the process work better.

Contact us when you need any support with this Self-Assessment and any help with templates, blue-prints and examples of standard documents you might need:

http://theartofservice.com
service@theartofservice.com

Included Resources - how to access

Included with your purchase of the book is the Situational

Leadership Self-Assessment Spreadsheet Dashboard which contains all questions and Self-Assessment areas and auto-generates insights, graphs, and project RACI planning - all with examples to get you started right away.

How? Simply send an email to
access@theartofservice.com
with this books' title in the subject to get the Situational Leadership Self Assessment Tool right away.

You will receive the following contents with New and Updated specific criteria:

- The latest quick edition of the book in PDF

- The latest complete edition of the book in PDF, which criteria correspond to the criteria in...

- The Self-Assessment Excel Dashboard, and...

- Example pre-filled Self-Assessment Excel Dashboard to get familiar with results generation

- In-depth specific Checklists covering the topic

- Project management checklists and templates to assist with implementation

INCLUDES LIFETIME SELF ASSESSMENT UPDATES

Every self assessment comes with Lifetime Updates and Lifetime Free Updated Books. Lifetime Updates is an industry-first feature which allows you to receive verified self assessment updates, ensuring you always have the most accurate information at your fingertips.

Get it now- you will be glad you did - do it now, before you forget.

Send an email to **access@theartofservice.com** with this books' title in the subject to get the Situational Leadership Self Assessment Tool right away.

Purpose of this Self-Assessment

This Self-Assessment has been developed to improve understanding of the requirements and elements of Situational Leadership, based on best practices and standards in business process architecture, design and quality management.

It is designed to allow for a rapid Self-Assessment to determine how closely existing management practices and procedures correspond to the elements of the Self-Assessment.

The criteria of requirements and elements of Situational Leadership have been rephrased in the format of a Self-Assessment questionnaire, with a seven-criterion scoring system, as explained in this document.

In this format, even with limited background knowledge of Situational Leadership, a manager can quickly review existing operations to determine how they measure up to the standards. This in turn can serve as the starting point of a 'gap analysis' to identify management tools or system elements that might usefully be implemented in the organization to help improve overall performance.

How to use the Self-Assessment

On the following pages are a series of questions to identify to what extent your Situational Leadership initiative is complete in comparison to the requirements set in standards.

To facilitate answering the questions, there is a space in front of each question to enter a score on a scale of '1' to '5'.

1 Strongly Disagree

2 Disagree

3 Neutral

4 Agree

5 Strongly Agree

Read the question and rate it with the following in front of mind:

'In my belief,
the answer to this question is clearly defined'.

There are two ways in which you can choose to interpret this statement;
1. how aware are you that the answer to the question is clearly defined
2. for more in-depth analysis you can choose to gather evidence and confirm the answer to the question. This obviously will take more time, most Self-Assessment users opt for the first way to interpret the question and dig deeper later on based on the outcome of the overall Self-Assessment.

A score of '1' would mean that the answer is not clear at all, where a '5' would mean the answer is crystal clear and defined. Leave emtpy when the question is not applicable or you don't want to answer it, you can skip it without affecting your score. Write your score in the space provided.

After you have responded to all the appropriate statements in each section, compute your average score for that section, using the formula provided, and round to the nearest tenth. Then transfer to the corresponding spoke in the Situational Leadership Scorecard on the second next page of the Self-Assessment.

Your completed Situational Leadership Scorecard will give you a clear presentation of which Situational Leadership areas need attention.

Situational Leadership Scorecard Example

Example of how the finalized Scorecard can look like:

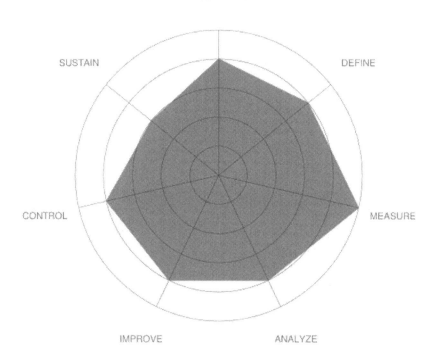

Situational Leadership Scorecard

Your Scores:

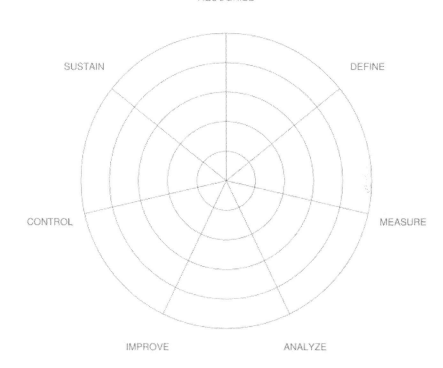

BEGINNING OF THE SELF-ASSESSMENT:

CRITERION #1: RECOGNIZE

INTENT: Be aware of the need for change. Recognize that there is an unfavorable variation, problem or symptom.

In my belief, the answer to this question is clearly defined:

5 Strongly Agree

4 Agree

3 Neutral

2 Disagree

1 Strongly Disagree

1. What would happen if Situational Leadership weren't done?
<--- Score

2. Has leadership addressed staff culture issues, training needs and attitudes?
<--- Score

3. What are your specific needs in regard to

leading and managing a quality program?
<--- Score

4. Are key stakeholders and organization leadership apprised of the concrete need for change and action?
<--- Score

5. What is the situation that would lead someone to need what you sell?
<--- Score

6. What are the stakeholder objectives to be achieved with Situational Leadership?
<--- Score

7. Why is the Manager-Director Transition so Problematic?
<--- Score

8. How do you ensure leaders identify the most critical future relationships?
<--- Score

9. Are there any specific expectations or concerns about the Situational Leadership team, Situational Leadership itself?
<--- Score

10. Who would you identify as a Highly Effective Leader?
<--- Score

11. What are the expected benefits of Situational Leadership to the stakeholder?
<--- Score

12. Do you identify conflict in your own situation as an opinion leader?
<--- Score

13. Has your organization identified a senior (lead) independent director?
<--- Score

14. What problems are you facing and how do you consider Situational Leadership will circumvent those obstacles?
<--- Score

15. What is the easiest, most direct way to solve the problem?
<--- Score

16. What are the key events that would represent the romantic perspective of leadership?
<--- Score

17. What are the operational issues that concern your organizations leadership?
<--- Score

18. What are the the key events that would represent the romantic perspective of leadership?
<--- Score

19. What was the best recognition you ever had in a work situation?
<--- Score

20. How are you going to measure success?
<--- Score

21. Has your organization identified a Senior Independent or Lead Director?
<--- Score

22. How do you ensure that leaders identify the most critical and relevant theme for unit?
<--- Score

23. What budget information needs to be included in the letters of support?
<--- Score

24. What skills and attributes do board directors need to work together as a leadership team?
<--- Score

25. How can do leaders adapt styles to meet the needs of different situations?
<--- Score

26. What does Situational Leadership success mean to the stakeholders?
<--- Score

27. What do you need to be an effective leader?
<--- Score

28. Are there procedures for employees reporting security problems and addressing the situation?
<--- Score

29. Can the present executive director accomplish the actions or does your organization need outside help?
<--- Score

30. What are the qualities you would need to use when being a coaching style leader?
<--- Score

31. Has your organization identified a lead/senior independent director?
<--- Score

32. Have you identified one or more persons on your staff with the potential to be the future Executive Director of your organization?
<--- Score

33. Who else hopes to benefit from it?
<--- Score

34. How can funders identify situations when networks are most powerful at achieving long-term change?
<--- Score

35. Are you in a position to leave all the space needed to the new director?
<--- Score

36. What situation(s) led to this Situational Leadership Self Assessment?
<--- Score

37. What assistance do you need to change the situation?
<--- Score

38. How would you address the situation with the members of each side of the issue?

<--- Score

39. Do you need your direct managers approval and support to participate?
<--- Score

40. How are the Situational Leadership's objectives aligned to the group's overall stakeholder strategy?
<--- Score

41. Does the product/commodity supply meet the needs (in cases of peaks and in normal situations)?
<--- Score

42. As a sponsor, customer or management, how important is it to meet goals, objectives?
<--- Score

43. How do self-directed teams manage the potential problem of diffusion of responsibility?
<--- Score

44. Did pod director communicate anticipated needs with section leaders?
<--- Score

45. What needs to be changed (and who needs to lead that change) to make the situation better?
<--- Score

46. How much style flex and breadth do you need to adapt to changing situational demands?
<--- Score

47. Who is the first point of contact in the event of a change in the executive directors situation?

<--- Score

48. How do you regularly recognize and reward team members who support other functions or business units?
<--- Score

49. When did the event/situation occur, or when will it occur?
<--- Score

50. What urgent and compelling issues are you directly addressing?
<--- Score

51. What need, challenge, or situation prompted you to choose it?
<--- Score

52. What are the attributes a leader needs for coaching, mentoring and guiding others?
<--- Score

53. Are we, collectively, good at recognizing and supporting different kinds of leadership?
<--- Score

54. Has your organization identified a Senior Independent Director or an independent Lead Director?
<--- Score

55. How have you been supporting employees ability to think and problem solve with your instruction?
<--- Score

56. How much are sponsors, customers, partners, stakeholders involved in Situational Leadership? In other words, what are the risks, if Situational Leadership does not deliver successfully?
<--- Score

57. Is it necessary for an outside consultant or a group facilitator to inform the current director and the board about issues that need to be addressed prior to the directors departure?
<--- Score

Add up total points for this section:
_____ = Total points for this section

Divided by: _____ (number of statements answered) = _____
Average score for this section

Transfer your score to the Situational Leadership Index at the beginning of the Self-Assessment.

CRITERION #2: DEFINE:

INTENT: Formulate the stakeholder problem. Define the problem, needs and objectives.

In my belief, the answer to this question is clearly defined:

5 Strongly Agree

4 Agree

3 Neutral

2 Disagree

1 Strongly Disagree

1. Is there a completed, verified, and validated high-level 'as is' (not 'should be' or 'could be') stakeholder process map?
<--- Score

2. When is/was the Situational Leadership start date?
<--- Score

3. Are different versions of process maps needed to

account for the different types of inputs?

<--- Score

4. How does the Situational Leadership manager ensure against scope creep?

<--- Score

5. Are transformational directors required for satisfied agents?

<--- Score

6. Are customers identified and high impact areas defined?

<--- Score

7. Has a team charter been developed and communicated?

<--- Score

8. Is there a completed SIPOC representation, describing the Suppliers, Inputs, Process, Outputs, and Customers?

<--- Score

9. What is strategic business unit and what type of leadership is required?

<--- Score

10. Is the team formed and are team leaders (Coaches and Management Leads) assigned?

<--- Score

11. Is the Situational Leadership scope manageable?

<--- Score

12. Are stakeholder processes mapped?

<--- Score

13. Are customer(s) identified and segmented according to their different needs and requirements?
<--- Score

14. Have the customer needs been translated into specific, measurable requirements? How?
<--- Score

15. How has your definition of leadership changed?
<--- Score

16. Is the improvement team aware of the different versions of a process: what they think it is vs. what it actually is vs. what it should be vs. what it could be?
<--- Score

17. What critical content must be communicated – who, what, when, where, and how?
<--- Score

18. Has the improvement team collected the 'voice of the customer' (obtained feedback – qualitative and quantitative)?
<--- Score

19. Is the current 'as is' process being followed? If not, what are the discrepancies?
<--- Score

20. How is the team tracking and documenting its work?
<--- Score

21. Has anyone else (internal or external to the group) attempted to solve this problem or a similar one before? If so, what knowledge can be leveraged from these previous efforts?
<--- Score

22. How flexible are you in modifying your dominant leadership style in situations that require a different style?
<--- Score

23. Are team charters developed?
<--- Score

24. What is the definition of leadership?
<--- Score

25. Are there different segments of customers?
<--- Score

26. Do senior managers actively promote the code and lead by example with regard to ethical conduct?
<--- Score

27. If substitutes have been appointed, have they been briefed on the Situational Leadership goals and received regular communications as to the progress to date?
<--- Score

28. Is Situational Leadership currently on schedule according to the plan?
<--- Score

29. Is Situational Leadership linked to key stakeholder

goals and objectives?
<--- Score

30. When are meeting minutes sent out? Who is on the distribution list?
<--- Score

31. What key stakeholder process output measure(s) does Situational Leadership leverage and how?
<--- Score

32. Has the board adopted a board leadership structure that ensures that the independent directors have a clearly defined leader?
<--- Score

33. How do you truly define the role of a leader in any organization, what are the characteristic of the already stated individuals and its organizational culture?
<--- Score

34. Has/have the customer(s) been identified?
<--- Score

35. How will variation in the actual durations of each activity be dealt with to ensure that the expected Situational Leadership results are met?
<--- Score

36. Has everyone on the team, including the team leaders, been properly trained?
<--- Score

37. Are improvement team members fully trained on Situational Leadership?

<--- Score

38. Is the team sponsored by a champion or stakeholder leader?
<--- Score

39. How will the Situational Leadership team and the group measure complete success of Situational Leadership?
<--- Score

40. When is the estimated completion date?
<--- Score

41. Is there regularly 100% attendance at the team meetings? If not, have appointed substitutes attended to preserve cross-functionality and full representation?
<--- Score

42. What life situations require brainstorming?
<--- Score

43. Who can forget the emblematic examples of market leaders missing the digital transformation?
<--- Score

44. How would the already stated skill requirements affect key relationship requirements for the future leader?
<--- Score

45. Is the team adequately staffed with the desired cross-functionality? If not, what additional resources are available to the team?
<--- Score

46. How would business leadership requirements interface with the professional and educational requirements for site administrators and directors?
<--- Score

47. Does the team have regular meetings?
<--- Score

48. Will team members regularly document their Situational Leadership work?
<--- Score

49. Is the team equipped with available and reliable resources?
<--- Score

50. How did the Situational Leadership manager receive input to the development of a Situational Leadership improvement plan and the estimated completion dates/times of each activity?
<--- Score

51. Is data collected and displayed to better understand customer(s) critical needs and requirements.
<--- Score

52. What training and coaching will be required across your organization?
<--- Score

53. What are the rough order estimates on cost savings/opportunities that Situational Leadership brings?

<--- Score

54. What are the boundaries of the scope? What is in bounds and what is not? What is the start point? What is the stop point?
<--- Score

55. What constraints exist that might impact the team?
<--- Score

56. What is your typical reaction to situations that require you to change a behavior or a practice?
<--- Score

57. Has a project plan, Gantt chart, or similar been developed/completed?
<--- Score

58. Are there any constraints known that bear on the ability to perform Situational Leadership work? How is the team addressing them?
<--- Score

59. What are the dynamics of the communication plan?
<--- Score

60. Will team members perform Situational Leadership work when assigned and in a timely fashion?
<--- Score

61. Who are the Situational Leadership improvement team members, including Management Leads and Coaches?

<--- Score

62. Is there a critical path to deliver Situational Leadership results?
<--- Score

63. Has a high-level 'as is' process map been completed, verified and validated?
<--- Score

64. How well does your team define and communicate a vision and direction for your organizations technology?
<--- Score

65. What is the business case to start direct channel (eCommerce) operations?
<--- Score

66. How do you keep key subject matter experts in the loop?
<--- Score

67. Has the Situational Leadership work been fairly and/or equitably divided and delegated among team members who are qualified and capable to perform the work? Has everyone contributed?
<--- Score

68. Is there a Situational Leadership management charter, including stakeholder case, problem and goal statements, scope, milestones, roles and responsibilities, communication plan?
<--- Score

69. What customer feedback methods were used to

solicit their input?

<--- Score

70. How was the 'as is' process map developed, reviewed, verified and validated?

<--- Score

71. Do the problem and goal statements meet the SMART criteria (specific, measurable, attainable, relevant, and time-bound)?

<--- Score

72. Are the purpose, direction, and approach defined and documented clearly?

<--- Score

73. What are the Roles and Responsibilities for each team member and its leadership? Where is this documented?

<--- Score

74. What activities require the largest amount of cross-team support?

<--- Score

75. How often are the team meetings?

<--- Score

76. What specifically is the problem? Where does it occur? When does it occur? What is its extent?

<--- Score

77. What are the compelling stakeholder reasons for embarking on Situational Leadership?

<--- Score

78. Has the direction changed at all during the course of Situational Leadership? If so, when did it change and why?
<--- Score

79. Is full participation by members in regularly held team meetings guaranteed?
<--- Score

80. What would be the goal or target for a Situational Leadership's improvement team?
<--- Score

81. Is a fully trained team formed, supported, and committed to work on the Situational Leadership improvements?
<--- Score

82. Are there select use cases you want to incubate and lead for your organization or business?
<--- Score

83. Is organizational coaching being examined specifically as a change leadership initiative?
<--- Score

Add up total points for this section:
_ _ _ _ _ = Total points for this section

Divided by: _ _ _ _ _ _ (number of statements answered) = _ _ _ _ _ _ Average score for this section

Transfer your score to the Situational Leadership Index at the beginning of the Self-Assessment.

CRITERION #3: MEASURE:

In my belief, the answer to this
question is clearly defined:

5 Strongly Agree

4 Agree

3 Neutral

2 Disagree

1 Strongly Disagree

1. What policies directly impact your innovation process/results?
<--- Score

2. Is there a Performance Baseline?
<--- Score

3. How does the leader impact the direction?
<--- Score

4. How is ethical leadership measured?

<--- Score

5. What are the trends in terms of direct business impacts?

<--- Score

6. How many people in organization are directly impacted by the project?

<--- Score

7. Where do you direct your efforts in order to make a meaningful impact?

<--- Score

8. Are key measures identified and agreed upon?

<--- Score

9. Who participated in the data collection for measurements?

<--- Score

10. How often do you consider measures with Executive leadership?

<--- Score

11. Why is there so much focus on transparency and direction?

<--- Score

12. How can directors get more involved in organization strategy and the impact of emerging technologies?

<--- Score

13. How large is the gap between current performance and the customer-specified (goal) performance?
<--- Score

14. What are the items or situations that cause you temptation?
<--- Score

15. Does a leaders opinion of subordinates have an impact on performance?
<--- Score

16. Do you turn your costly conflicts into positive situations that lead to beneficial results?
<--- Score

17. Are local leaders able to ensure that resources are directed to shared priorities, and are sustainable in the long term?
<--- Score

18. What are the key input variables? What are the key process variables? What are the key output variables?
<--- Score

19. Is long term and short term variability accounted for?
<--- Score

20. Is data collected on key measures that were identified?
<--- Score

21. What can be assumed to be the failure, which would act as cause leading to the hazardous

situation?
<--- Score

22. Have you found any 'ground fruit' or 'low-hanging fruit' for immediate remedies to the gap in performance?
<--- Score

23. What charts has the team used to display the components of variation in the process?
<--- Score

24. What are the expected direct impacts on employee outcomes?
<--- Score

25. What are the agreed upon definitions of the high impact areas, defect(s), unit(s), and opportunities that will figure into the process capability metrics?
<--- Score

26. Was a data collection plan established?
<--- Score

27. Is key measure data collection planned and executed, process variation displayed and communicated and performance baselined?
<--- Score

28. Is a solid data collection plan established that includes measurement systems analysis?
<--- Score

29. How does coaching impact personal leadership?
<--- Score

30. What particular quality tools did the team find helpful in establishing measurements?
<--- Score

31. Are business leaders focusing on short-term targets over long-term profitability?
<--- Score

32. What key measures identified indicate the performance of the stakeholder process?
<--- Score

33. Are high impact defects defined and identified in the stakeholder process?
<--- Score

34. Is there is a danger that too much openness and self-organization in the workplace could lead to disorganization, confusion, and lack of focus and direction?
<--- Score

35. What circumstances and underlying causes would turn an awkward situation into an unsustainable one?
<--- Score

36. Will the decision directly impact most subordinates?
<--- Score

37. How can the susceptibility analysis be designed to lead directly to management?
<--- Score

38. Is data collection planned and executed?
<--- Score

39. What data was collected (past, present, future/ongoing)?
<--- Score

40. What has the team done to assure the stability and accuracy of the measurement process?
<--- Score

41. How do you measure the ROI on your organizations coaching efforts?
<--- Score

42. How might long tenure impact the effectiveness of executives in role as strategic leaders?
<--- Score

43. How far do you believe that trust causes the leader to behave in an ethical way?
<--- Score

44. What type of coaching/support makes an impact?
<--- Score

45. Does direct mail really impact the environment as much as you are lead to believe?
<--- Score

46. What would you change about leadership focus or direction in your organization?
<--- Score

47. What life situations have caused the greatest growth for you?
<--- Score

48. What organizational priorities does your team have the capacity to support?
<--- Score

49. What does your organizations senior leader and direct reports personally do to create and maintain an environment for improving quality/ mission performance and customer focus?
<--- Score

50. Are process variation components displayed/ communicated using suitable charts, graphs, plots?
<--- Score

51. Who is directly impacted by the project?
<--- Score

52. Is Process Variation Displayed/Communicated?
<--- Score

53. What are the costs associated with leadership coaching?
<--- Score

54. Will the decision directly impact only a select few?
<--- Score

55. Does the vision provide focus and direction to the already stated who must make ongoing decisions?
<--- Score

56. Why measure return on investment obtained from leadership coaching?

<--- Score

57. What business outcomes will marketing directly impact?

<--- Score

58. What situational factors impact on the work of middle leaders?

<--- Score

59. Where should your organization focus its leadership development efforts?

<--- Score

Add up total points for this section:
_ _ _ _ _ = Total points for this section

Divided by: _ _ _ _ _ _ (number of statements answered) = _ _ _ _ _ _
Average score for this section

Transfer your score to the Situational Leadership Index at the beginning of the Self-Assessment.

CRITERION #4: ANALYZE:

INTENT: Analyze causes, assumptions
and hypotheses.

In my belief, the answer to this
question is clearly defined:

5 Strongly Agree

4 Agree

3 Neutral

2 Disagree

1 Strongly Disagree

1. Were there any improvement opportunities
identified from the process analysis?
<--- Score

**2. Which would be a direct output of the initiating
process group?**
<--- Score

**3. How often have you been asked, during the
selection process, to produce direct evidence of**

your qualifications and experience?
<--- Score

4. Does the board of directors play a leading role in the process of developing and reviewing your organizations strategy at least annually?
<--- Score

5. What tools were used to generate the list of possible causes?
<--- Score

6. Is there something that sits behind the strategy (data to support direction)?
<--- Score

7. Who will lead the change process?
<--- Score

8. Did any value-added analysis or 'lean thinking' take place to identify some of the gaps shown on the 'as is' process map?
<--- Score

9. What were the crucial 'moments of truth' on the process map?
<--- Score

10. Was a cause-and-effect diagram used to explore the different types of causes (or sources of variation)?
<--- Score

11. What is the leadership engagement process?
<--- Score

12. Who will be directly in charge of the various

stages of the process?
<--- Score

13. Have any additional benefits been identified that will result from closing all or most of the gaps?
<--- Score

14. What quality tools were used to get through the analyze phase?
<--- Score

15. Can opportunity be created for a different and possibly better situation tomorrow?
<--- Score

16. Are there ample opportunities for other business people to assume leadership roles in the partnership?
<--- Score

17. How does the coaching process proceed?
<--- Score

18. Does your organization systematically track and analyze outcomes related for accountability and quality improvement?
<--- Score

19. Is there a good practice process for the selection of independent directors?
<--- Score

20. Is the Situational Leadership process severely broken such that a re-design is necessary?
<--- Score

21. Is the data architecture of your organization supportive of the scorecard?
<--- Score

22. Which stakeholder characteristics are analyzed?
<--- Score

23. Have the problem and goal statements been updated to reflect the additional knowledge gained from the analyze phase?
<--- Score

24. What projects do you delegate that would be valuable development opportunities for others?
<--- Score

25. How do you provide leadership and growth opportunities for staff?
<--- Score

26. Have all non-recommended alternatives been analyzed in sufficient detail?
<--- Score

27. Who may appoint the Acting or Interim Executive Director/What process must take place?
<--- Score

28. How was the detailed process map generated, verified, and validated?
<--- Score

29. Are pertinent alerts monitored, analyzed and distributed to appropriate personnel?
<--- Score

30. What tools were used to narrow the list of possible causes?
<--- Score

31. Is the performance gap determined?
<--- Score

32. Are you ready to connect the people, processes, and information needed to manage all direct and indirect sourcing categories and activities in a simple, smart, and open way?
<--- Score

33. What is the cost of poor quality as supported by the team's analysis?
<--- Score

34. Does Situational Leadership systematically track and analyze outcomes for accountability and quality improvement?
<--- Score

35. Have changes been properly/adequately analyzed for effect?
<--- Score

36. What do model practices, benchmarking, fair rate-setting practices, leadership and a stable, qualified direct support workforce have in common?
<--- Score

37. Is the gap/opportunity displayed and communicated in financial terms?
<--- Score

38. What conclusions were drawn from the team's data collection and analysis? How did the team reach these conclusions?

<--- Score

39. What role do strategic leaders play in the strategic management process?

<--- Score

40. What better way for Directors to demonstrate performance and accountability than an annual appraisal process?

<--- Score

41. Were Pareto charts (or similar) used to portray the 'heavy hitters' (or key sources of variation)?

<--- Score

42. Are acquisition and investment opportunities setting the direction of your organization?

<--- Score

43. How can one support the decision-making process leading to a situated method?

<--- Score

44. Have you kept your leadership informed and part of the process?

<--- Score

45. What does the data say about the performance of the stakeholder process?

<--- Score

46. Are there situations and events that lead to

entropy processes inside your organization?

<--- Score

47. What are the revised rough estimates of the financial savings/opportunity for Situational Leadership improvements?

<--- Score

48. How do you identify and analyze stakeholders and their interests?

<--- Score

49. Who has the responsibility for directly managing the total stream across your organization, to connect the maps and lead the improvement process?

<--- Score

50. Are losses documented, analyzed, and remedial processes developed to prevent future losses?

<--- Score

51. What processes apply to obtaining letters of support?

<--- Score

52. Have the types of risks that may impact Situational Leadership been identified and analyzed?

<--- Score

53. Have the concerns of stakeholders to help identify and define potential barriers been obtained and analyzed?

<--- Score

54. Are contracting directors or chiefs adequately qualified/certified?
<--- Score

55. Are there things that you do to give away your data directly, or are there certain signs that would lead a prudent adversary to deduce your data (indicators or clues)?
<--- Score

56. What are your key Situational Leadership indicators that you will measure, analyze and track?
<--- Score

57. Were any designed experiments used to generate additional insight into the data analysis?
<--- Score

58. Are gaps between current performance and the goal performance identified?
<--- Score

59. How will the Situational Leadership data be analyzed?
<--- Score

60. What were the financial benefits resulting from any 'ground fruit or low-hanging fruit' (quick fixes)?
<--- Score

61. Is the coaching process a blanket approach for the leader, or customized?
<--- Score

62. Is data and process analysis, root cause analysis and quantifying the gap/opportunity in place?
<--- Score

63. Did any additional data need to be collected?
<--- Score

64. Do staff have the necessary skills to collect, analyze, and report data?
<--- Score

65. What did the team gain from developing a sub-process map?
<--- Score

66. What kind of supporting data do you need?
<--- Score

67. Was a detailed process map created to amplify critical steps of the 'as is' stakeholder process?
<--- Score

Add up total points for this section:
_ _ _ _ _ = Total points for this section

Divided by: _ _ _ _ _ _ (number of statements answered) = _ _ _ _ _ _ Average score for this section

Transfer your score to the Situational Leadership Index at the beginning of the Self-Assessment.

CRITERION #5: IMPROVE:

INTENT: Develop a practical solution. Innovate, establish and test the solution and to measure the results.

In my belief, the answer to this question is clearly defined:

5 Strongly Agree

4 Agree

3 Neutral

2 Disagree

1 Strongly Disagree

1. Do directors develop and articulate risk appetite and risk culture?
<--- Score

2. Was a pilot designed for the proposed solution(s)?
<--- Score

3. What were the underlying assumptions on the cost-benefit analysis?

<--- Score

4. Does the board of directors engage in robust consideration about the top risks and is there agreement between management and the board about the most critical risks to your organization?
<--- Score

5. When might new or emerging risks shape or refine your organizations strategic direction?
<--- Score

6. Why did you decide to become a director?
<--- Score

7. Is it feasible that a successor be groomed, knowing that the final decision for the new executive director rests with the board of directors?
<--- Score

8. Have you gained a clear, detailed picture of the current situation and the areas for improvement?
<--- Score

9. Do directors direct and control risk-based decisions?
<--- Score

10. Has the facility implemented consumer satisfaction surveys, considered results with staff, and used results to direct revisions in service provision?
<--- Score

11. Is the solution leading you to the right

direction?
<--- Score

12. How did the leaders or groups principles direct the decision made?
<--- Score

13. Is the optimal solution selected based on testing and analysis?
<--- Score

14. How can different perspectives lead to a new understanding of the situation?
<--- Score

15. What attendant changes will need to be made to ensure that the solution is successful?
<--- Score

16. What does the 'should be' process map/design look like?
<--- Score

17. How well does your leader understand your teams relationship with other functions?
<--- Score

18. How do leaders make decisions about which skills to apply in any given situation requiring leadership?
<--- Score

19. What tools were used to tap into the creativity and encourage 'outside the box' thinking?
<--- Score

20. What is the implementation plan?
<--- Score

21. How do you establish the rules – authorities, decision rights and direction – across departments and organizations to manage threats?
<--- Score

22. Do you spend time coaching employees regarding ways to improve employee scores?
<--- Score

23. How can the potential tensions in developing coaching practice be mediated through effective leadership and management?
<--- Score

24. Is the result overwhelmingly tipped in one direction?
<--- Score

25. Do you have a clear understanding of your leaders current mind-sets?
<--- Score

26. What changes could be made to the overall system that may improve the situation?
<--- Score

27. How will you decide on a shared direction?
<--- Score

28. Is your senior team directly engaged in the leadership development of your organization?
<--- Score

29. Do you have systems in place whereby staff are able to understand disturbance situations and make an informed judgment as to severity?
<--- Score

30. How effective was your leadership coach in assisting you to identify development goals and objectives?
<--- Score

31. Are new and improved process ('should be') maps developed?
<--- Score

32. How does the solution remove the key sources of issues discovered in the analyze phase?
<--- Score

33. How does a team leader, manager, consultant or facilitator know what to attend to when attempting to intervene in a team in order to improve the situation?
<--- Score

34. What are the characteristics of the high-performing leaders that enable them to demonstrate critical behaviors more often, in more situations, and with better results?
<--- Score

35. How does executive coaching improve transformational leadership behaviours?
<--- Score

36. Who is leading future development direction?
<--- Score

37. What made a difference to your development as a leader?
<--- Score

38. What is the unit leadership doing to (maintain/ improve) the morale?
<--- Score

39. Are improved process ('should be') maps modified based on pilot data and analysis?
<--- Score

40. Were any criteria developed to assist the team in testing and evaluating potential solutions?
<--- Score

41. Is leadership development fit for purpose?
<--- Score

42. Is pilot data collected and analyzed?
<--- Score

43. Is executive leadership and/or management involved in risk management and mitigation decisions?
<--- Score

44. What tools were used to evaluate the potential solutions?
<--- Score

45. How did you help make complex ideas or situations more clear or understandable?
<--- Score

46. Is a contingency plan established?
<--- Score

47. What happens when you try to do leadership development without coaching?
<--- Score

48. How do you improve the situation?
<--- Score

49. What is Situational Leadership's impact on utilizing the best solution(s)?
<--- Score

50. How much senior leadership time is dedicated to supporting frontline staff in trialling innovations and delivering improvements?
<--- Score

51. What could have been most improved regarding the Executive Directors performance in the past year?
<--- Score

52. Are there any constraints (technical, political, cultural, or otherwise) that would inhibit certain solutions?
<--- Score

53. What can leaders do to improve situation?
<--- Score

54. Are the benefits of coaching established within the senior leadership team, and is there a clear rationale for coaching as a result?
<--- Score

55. Is the executive leadership in support of the solution?

<--- Score

56. Are you mostly looking for information about how the system works, about how to develop your leadership competencies, or about how to handle a particularly challenging situation?

<--- Score

57. What are the situational characteristics that developed them into leaders?

<--- Score

58. What situational risk factors apply?

<--- Score

59. Are possible solutions generated and tested?

<--- Score

60. Is there a cost/benefit analysis of optimal solution(s)?

<--- Score

61. How will the team or the process owner(s) monitor the implementation plan to see that it is working as intended?

<--- Score

62. What is the team's contingency plan for potential problems occurring in implementation?

<--- Score

63. What is optimal leadership style?

<--- Score

64. What error proofing will be done to address some of the discrepancies observed in the 'as is' process?
<--- Score

65. How do you improve your style capabilities to fit a broader array of situational demands?
<--- Score

66. When can coaching techniques be used to develop the team?
<--- Score

67. Is the board satisfied that its current complement of directors has the requisite expertise and industry knowledge to provide effective oversight of your organizations most critical risks?
<--- Score

68. How do you improve your conflict management techniques for future situations?
<--- Score

69. What risk control measures are already in place, or need to be in place to assure that hazardous situations wont occur or wont lead to a harmful conclusion?
<--- Score

70. What tools were most useful during the improve phase?
<--- Score

71. How did it feel to reach resolution to leadership situations using you messages?

<--- Score

72. Is there a small-scale pilot for proposed improvement(s)? What conclusions were drawn from the outcomes of a pilot?
<--- Score

73. Are the right leaders following the development of the technology and protocols?
<--- Score

74. How do successful companies develop leaders?
<--- Score

75. What were the situations the resolution was intended to resolve?
<--- Score

76. What hazards, including human limitations and situational risk factors, might be present?
<--- Score

77. How can leadership position itself to best support the already stated people and allowing leadership to understand what role is in bubbling up that talent and supporting that talent going forward?
<--- Score

78. Can principal leadership be improved through feedback and coaching?
<--- Score

79. How did the team generate the list of possible solutions?
<--- Score

80. What skills in leadership, decision making and communication are important for being a member of a board of directors?
<--- Score

81. Does your board ensure strong leadership and a clear strategic direction developed with input from all team members within your organization?
<--- Score

82. Is the implementation plan designed?
<--- Score

83. Who is directing the use of Risk Management?
<--- Score

84. Are your direct mail specialists given room to develop own direction?
<--- Score

85. Who is driving and leading the business case development for your organization?
<--- Score

86. What lessons, if any, from a pilot were incorporated into the design of the full-scale solution?
<--- Score

87. Have you set measurable improvement goals in line with the business direction?
<--- Score

88. How effective was your leadership coach at supporting you to achieve your identified development goals and objectives?

<--- Score

89. How are you developing your organizational capacity and capability for developing and supporting leadership and quality improvement methods?
<--- Score

90. Is a high-level policy decision needed to resolve a situation?
<--- Score

91. How does a coaching approach support the development of leadership capacity and capability in your organization?
<--- Score

92. Describe the design of the pilot and what tests were conducted, if any?
<--- Score

93. How did you deal with the situation and what was the result?
<--- Score

94. How does the solution support your organizations long term goals?
<--- Score

95. Is a solution implementation plan established, including schedule/work breakdown structure, resources, risk management plan, cost/budget, and control plan?
<--- Score

96. What are the maximum capacities of inbound

flows in the optimal situation?
<--- Score

97. How much direct influence do employees have on organization decisions?
<--- Score

98. How do the leaders of organizations achieve results?
<--- Score

99. Do you embed information directly into your product as a functional capability or a decision aid?
<--- Score

100. What communications are necessary to support the implementation of the solution?
<--- Score

101. Has decision making been tested when leading a team outside of area of expertise and in situations of great complexity and ambiguity?
<--- Score

102. Why should your organization invest in developing the leadership within its ranks?
<--- Score

103. How will the group know that the solution worked?
<--- Score

104. How do you ensure your organization has the capacity and capability for developing leadership and supporting quality improvement?

<--- Score

105. Did your investment accrue tangible and intangible results leading to better business outcomes?
<--- Score

106. Are the best solutions selected?
<--- Score

Add up total points for this section:
_ _ _ _ _ = Total points for this section

Divided by: _ _ _ _ _ _ (number of statements answered) = _ _ _ _ _ _
Average score for this section

Transfer your score to the Situational Leadership Index at the beginning of the Self-Assessment.

CRITERION #6: CONTROL:

INTENT: Implement the practical solution. Maintain the performance and correct possible complications.

In my belief, the answer to this question is clearly defined:

5 Strongly Agree

4 Agree

3 Neutral

2 Disagree

1 Strongly Disagree

1. Are you implementing the correct approach to deal with the specific situation rather than just simply following pre-determined plans?
<--- Score

2. Are operating procedures consistent?
<--- Score

3. Does job training on the documented procedures

need to be part of the process team's education and training?
<--- Score

4. How successful have leaders been in rallying widespread support for employment as a priority?
<--- Score

5. What other systems, operations, processes, and infrastructures (hiring practices, staffing, training, incentives/rewards, metrics/dashboards/scorecards, etc.) need updates, additions, changes, or deletions in order to facilitate knowledge transfer and improvements?
<--- Score

6. What other areas of the group might benefit from the Situational Leadership team's improvements, knowledge, and learning?
<--- Score

7. Is new knowledge gained imbedded in the response plan?
<--- Score

8. How might the group capture best practices and lessons learned so as to leverage improvements?
<--- Score

9. Who will support you in learning processes?
<--- Score

10. Do you have the right leadership and facilitating mechanisms for supporting inter-organization contingency planning?
<--- Score

11. How could manufacturers use the improved demand visibility to improve planning in situations when lead-times and capacity, at least in theory, would allow a manufacturer to react to market demand?
<--- Score

12. How does pulling rank reflect more on the leader than on the situation?
<--- Score

13. What other possible explanations for the current situation might there be?
<--- Score

14. Is a response plan established and deployed?
<--- Score

15. What have you learned about allocating resources when in a leadership situation?
<--- Score

16. Is reporting being used or needed?
<--- Score

17. How will new or emerging customer needs/requirements be checked/communicated to orient the process toward meeting the new specifications and continually reducing variation?
<--- Score

18. Is a response plan in place for when the input, process, or output measures indicate an 'out-of-control' condition?
<--- Score

19. Are suggested corrective/restorative actions indicated on the response plan for known causes to problems that might surface?
<--- Score

20. Do you plan to retire upon leaving your current position as Executive Director?
<--- Score

21. How will the process owner and team be able to hold the gains?
<--- Score

22. What is the recommended frequency of auditing?
<--- Score

23. How do you know if your project has succeeded against the already stated goals, or whether were heading in the right direction?
<--- Score

24. Is the vision of the leader or does it reflect the situation?
<--- Score

25. What is how you and/or others stepped back from the situation and reflected on how the previous success or failure might apply?
<--- Score

26. Has the improved process and its steps been standardized?
<--- Score

27. How do you control a situation that has been

viewed subjectively, vaguely, and inconsistently?
<--- Score

28. How much of leadership is about control, delegation and theater?
<--- Score

29. Are documented procedures clear and easy to follow for the operators?
<--- Score

30. Will the director of the pmo have a disproportionate amount of control?
<--- Score

31. How do the potential changes reflect your organizations direction and vision?
<--- Score

32. What are the critical parameters to watch?
<--- Score

33. Is leadership committed to high standards of ethical behavior?
<--- Score

34. How will the day-to-day responsibilities for monitoring and continual improvement be transferred from the improvement team to the process owner?
<--- Score

35. Can literacy coaching provide a model for organization-wide professional learning?
<--- Score

36. Are plans to collect inputs and related analysis of actual situations defined in the procedure?
<--- Score

37. Does the Situational Leadership performance meet the customer's requirements?
<--- Score

38. Is the risk reporting to the board balanced and does it reflect the present and potential future situation?
<--- Score

39. Are there situations where rational control leads to negative social affects?
<--- Score

40. How do you facilitate your leaders ability to see ahead in order to control direction, rather than being controlled by it?
<--- Score

41. Are there documented procedures?
<--- Score

42. What should the next improvement project be that is related to Situational Leadership?
<--- Score

43. Why should leaders do introspection and reflect on decisions?
<--- Score

44. Does the response plan contain a definite closed loop continual improvement scheme (e.g., plan-do-check-act)?

<--- Score

45. Are senior staff committed to leading implementation of the plan?
<--- Score

46. What is your plan for developing new leaders?
<--- Score

47. How do your current technology roadmap and capabilities compare against direct competitors and market leaders?
<--- Score

48. Do you have any direct or indirect control over foreign organization or other offshore accounts?
<--- Score

49. How will the process owner verify improvement in present and future sigma levels, process capabilities?
<--- Score

50. How certain are you that the situation is under control?
<--- Score

51. Which levels of integration often leads to strategic plans that your organization cannot successfully implement?
<--- Score

52. What quality tools were useful in the control phase?
<--- Score

53. Do the activities still serve a control purpose in

your current situation?
<--- Score

54. Is there a recommended audit plan for routine surveillance inspections of Situational Leadership's gains?
<--- Score

55. Is there a control plan in place for sustaining improvements (short and long-term)?
<--- Score

56. Do your policies reflect shifts in direction resulting from new leadership?
<--- Score

57. What is how you and/or others stepped back from the situation and reflected on why the project succeeded or failed?
<--- Score

58. Is there documentation that will support the successful operation of the improvement?
<--- Score

59. What have been important learning experiences that you have had, that were particularly useful for your professional development as a director?
<--- Score

60. What is the control/monitoring plan?
<--- Score

61. Is there a standardized process?
<--- Score

62. How will you spread the adoption of coaching as a leadership style used by leaders at all levels of your organization?

<--- Score

63. What types of leaders are most effective under various situational control?

<--- Score

64. Is the gut, the research, the determined consensus of the ones with the control levers clear about the direction well lead in and precisely why were doing it?

<--- Score

65. What are the standard lead times for the launching of new programs?

<--- Score

66. Will any special training be provided for results interpretation?

<--- Score

67. How can corporate learning programs more effectively develop leadership talent?

<--- Score

68. What key inputs and outputs are being measured on an ongoing basis?

<--- Score

69. Have new or revised work instructions resulted?

<--- Score

70. Is there a transfer of ownership and knowledge

to process owner and process team tasked with the responsibilities.
<--- Score

71. How will input, process, and output variables be checked to detect for sub-optimal conditions?
<--- Score

72. Who is the Situational Leadership process owner?
<--- Score

73. Does a troubleshooting guide exist or is it needed?
<--- Score

74. Is there a documented and implemented monitoring plan?
<--- Score

75. Does your organization have the leadership capacity to sustain the plan over time?
<--- Score

76. How will report readings be checked to effectively monitor performance?
<--- Score

77. Which step in the strategic planning process is to Develop an overarching vision and supporting mission to drive the strategic direction of your organization?
<--- Score

78. Is knowledge gained on process shared and institutionalized?
<--- Score

79. Is coaching/learning the best leadership style for your business?
<--- Score

80. How can senior leaders control (ensure uniformity of) the message?
<--- Score

81. Are new process steps, standards, and documentation ingrained into normal operations?
<--- Score

82. What would the impact of your thinking/ reflection be on the situation?
<--- Score

83. Do you have a formal plan for succession of your leadership roles and your board directors?
<--- Score

Add up total points for this section:
_ _ _ _ _ = Total points for this section

Divided by: _ _ _ _ _ _ (number of statements answered) = _ _ _ _ _ _
Average score for this section

Transfer your score to the Situational Leadership Index at the beginning of the Self-Assessment.

CRITERION #7: SUSTAIN:

INTENT: Retain the benefits.

In my belief, the answer to this question is clearly defined:

5 Strongly Agree

4 Agree

3 Neutral

2 Disagree

1 Strongly Disagree

1. What happened in that situation?
<--- Score

2. Is it organizational and directional?
<--- Score

3. Did you use the directory to locate resources?
<--- Score

4. How did you handle each situation?
<--- Score

5. Who is charged with management, implementation, and direction of all physical security programs?

<--- Score

6. Does your organization have adequate leadership and direction?

<--- Score

7. How well did you handle the already stated situations?

<--- Score

8. What kind of knowledge is most useful to project managers and teams and in what situations?

<--- Score

9. Is that the situation at your organization?

<--- Score

10. How does inclusion play a part in workload change situations?

<--- Score

11. Does a leader in your organization communicate reasons for strategic direction to stakeholders?

<--- Score

12. What happens in situations where there is no acceptance or disagreement about the direction the leaders are trying to take your organization?

<--- Score

13. What about it and business leaders?
<--- Score

14. What is the current organization vision and direction as set by the leadership team?
<--- Score

15. Can the management team achieve sufficient commitment to make a choice to change direction?
<--- Score

16. How can leaders influence followers?
<--- Score

17. What if the direct seller keeps your organizations products on hand to show to potential customers?
<--- Score

18. Why is functional diversity important to leadership at the strategic level?
<--- Score

19. Who should support the core functions of the research organization?
<--- Score

20. What would you do to respond to the situation?
<--- Score

21. Is it acceptable for ones values to change from situation to situation?
<--- Score

22. What is your current leadership situation?
<--- Score

23. How do fundraising programs and people make determinations in difficult (sometimes near-impossible) situations?
<--- Score

24. What are some situations where it would be important to use diplomatic language?
<--- Score

25. How do communication styles change in different situations?
<--- Score

26. How well does the senior team provide collective leadership and direction to your organization and how well does it implement change?
<--- Score

27. What is the current situation for workers making clothes?
<--- Score

28. What rules of thumb do you take away and apply to your own situation?
<--- Score

29. Has the program manager directed other projects of similar size and complexity?
<--- Score

30. How do particular situations and circumstances affect how your identity is perceived?

<--- Score

31. How do you apply what worked previously to the current situation?
<--- Score

32. Are your personal beliefs in line with organization direction and strategy?
<--- Score

33. Is your leadership heading in the right direction?
<--- Score

34. Is there executive leadership directing and accountable for telehealth services?
<--- Score

35. How does the leadership coaching program work?
<--- Score

36. Do you know direct and indirect spend trends for each part of your business?
<--- Score

37. How do leadership styles affect your organizations way of dealing with conflicts?
<--- Score

38. How do you build trust with your peers, direct reports, or supervisors?
<--- Score

39. What could derail the success of a new director?

<--- Score

40. Are you taking all of the right steps and heading in the right direction?
<--- Score

41. How likely are you to doze off or fall asleep in situations, in contrast to feeling just tired?
<--- Score

42. Are people seeking a particular form of leadership?
<--- Score

43. What are the skills that enable a competent architect as technical, social, leadership skills and situation-specific skill profiles?
<--- Score

44. How many times have you served as an Acting or Interim Executive Director?
<--- Score

45. What types of providers/support staff do you have to provide integration?
<--- Score

46. What is a leadership stretch for you?
<--- Score

47. Do leaders have direct or indirect effects on growth?
<--- Score

48. What leadership, mentoring and/or coaching roles are there (your managers do)?

<--- Score

49. Do the top executives have a clear and shared direction?
<--- Score

50. How do you apply a particular ethical principle to a specific life situation?
<--- Score

51. Where do great sales enablement leaders come from?
<--- Score

52. Does the board have a lead independent director?
<--- Score

53. Which channel works best in situations?
<--- Score

54. What are the outcomes that can be expected from effective strategic leadership?
<--- Score

55. Have you ever noticed a situation that could lead to a violent incident?
<--- Score

56. How will you use the idea of champions and coaching within your organization to implement your initiative?
<--- Score

57. What is servant leadership all about?
<--- Score

58. What outcomes comprise enterprise leadership?

<--- Score

59. Are directors clear about expectations?

<--- Score

60. How will you address the situation?

<--- Score

61. How can a leader increase the level of engagement and commitment amongst team players?

<--- Score

62. Why engage in leadership coaching?

<--- Score

63. Are there unrealistic expectations by the board and the staff for the next executive director?

<--- Score

64. What employee and related service professional behaviors lead to high quality inclusive practices?

<--- Score

65. What do you consider as the key to success for strategic leaders?

<--- Score

66. How have you proactively sought direct feedback on what gaps in your knowledge or skills may exist?

<--- Score

67. What are some situations where you might be called on to deliver an impromptu speech?
<--- Score

68. How much management oversight and direction are you ready to provide?
<--- Score

69. Is it any different than any other leadership situation?
<--- Score

70. What situations do your colleagues rely on you to handle?
<--- Score

71. How do senior leaders set organizational direction, vision, and values?
<--- Score

72. Is the change management leader deeply knowledgeable of field service operations and culture?
<--- Score

73. Can a leader really put everyone in in-group?
<--- Score

74. How much of that vision is about us, as leaders?
<--- Score

75. Does your organization bring leadership considerations into its strategic considerations even earlier, before it chooses a general direction?

<--- Score

76. Does your organization provide direct access to technology professionals?
<--- Score

77. How can the departing Executive Director make the leadership transition run smoothly?
<--- Score

78. Do scallops in the Winding Way help to indicate the original flow direction?
<--- Score

79. What does your competitive situation look like market leader in a segment?
<--- Score

80. What would directors look for if invited to join a board?
<--- Score

81. Is there clear leadership in determining the strategic direction of your organization?
<--- Score

82. Does it promote win/win situations?
<--- Score

83. What should local economic leaders do now to make the most of the situation?
<--- Score

84. What grounds are there for organization directors to make the already stated judgements on behalf?

<--- Score

85. What factors may lead to the derailment of leaders in your organization?
<--- Score

86. Do you receive hazard-warning messages directly from the lead organization?
<--- Score

87. Does the board have a strong independent chairperson or a lead director?
<--- Score

88. How do you know where in your range of behaviors to be in any given situation?
<--- Score

89. What exactly is the current situation?
<--- Score

90. How are leaders from other industries harnessing digital for competitive advantage?
<--- Score

91. How important is leader trustworthiness in establishing a positive climate?
<--- Score

92. Do you have what it take to solve the situation and break free?
<--- Score

93. How did you feel about the scheduled timing of the online leadership training?
<--- Score

94. What is threatening about the situation?
<--- Score

95. What are some ethical challenges that are unique to strategic leaders?
<--- Score

96. Are you leading your procurement organization in the right direction?
<--- Score

97. What are the obstacles leaders who govern are likely to experience in practicing or enabling leadership?
<--- Score

98. Do you have direct access to Business Intelligence (BI) systems in your current role?
<--- Score

99. Why is an executive director evaluation necessary?
<--- Score

100. How would power affect individuals who have the choice to engage in gossip in a conflict situation?
<--- Score

101. Do companies truly value diversity directors?
<--- Score

102. When has it been necessary for you to tolerate an ambiguous situation at work?
<--- Score

103. What are the situations that make acting with integrity difficult?
<--- Score

104. Which leadership style is right for you?
<--- Score

105. Are there situations where servant leadership is inappropriate and a different leadership approach would be more effective?
<--- Score

106. What specifically did the leadership team see that made them convinced that moving to a value-based footing was the direction to go?
<--- Score

107. Do you have continued senior leadership support for facing ongoing challenges?
<--- Score

108. What is the nature of the situation?
<--- Score

109. What final conclusions can one draw about the role of situations in leadership?
<--- Score

110. How can employees facilitate employee-directed small groups and independent work?
<--- Score

111. Is anyone with a conflict of interest guiding or directing the compliance and ethics program?
<--- Score

112. What constraints apply to the situation?
<--- Score

113. How well does the senior team provide collective leadership and direction to your organization?
<--- Score

114. Does your organization have communications channels that work effectively in all directions?
<--- Score

115. What would oversight of the CEO/Executive Director look like?
<--- Score

116. What else is going on that might be affecting the situation?
<--- Score

117. What is the effect of being exposed to other leadership training?
<--- Score

118. How exactly do you create new organizational capabilities and supporting leadership behaviors?
<--- Score

119. What can directories and lead aggregators do for your business?
<--- Score

120. How do interventions as coaching, goal setting, and training complement and reinforce leadership change?

<--- Score

121. Can leading brands succeed in a world that is inherently about choice and personalization?
<--- Score

122. How do leaders know which leadership skills to use in which situations to achieve goals and objectives?
<--- Score

123. Do board members have the right mix of skills to lead and direct?
<--- Score

124. Do communications lead to a common operating picture and situational awareness?
<--- Score

125. What is the role of the outgoing director during the transition?
<--- Score

126. What is the current situation regarding the supply of the internal sequencing flow?
<--- Score

127. Are you a project manager or a manager/ director?
<--- Score

128. What leadership weaknesses did you observe?
<--- Score

129. How does the strategic leader of the

profession lead the profession?

<--- Score

130. What leadership, mentoring and/or coaching roles are there (you do)?

<--- Score

131. What are the best features of the current situation that could be built on to make things much better?

<--- Score

132. What aspects is a part in your daily work as a leader?

<--- Score

133. What is a truly meaningful life direction?

<--- Score

134. What should be the Executive Directors performance goals for the next year?

<--- Score

135. Will the senior executive leadership capability framework be changed over time?

<--- Score

136. Have you faced any similar situations?

<--- Score

137. What is the basis of charismatic leadership?

<--- Score

138. How do senior executives and organizational directors take the appropriate actions to defend shareholders?

<--- Score

139. How can companies choose a direction amid all the digital noise?
<--- Score

140. Have you ever been in a situation that has gotten out of hand due to anger?
<--- Score

141. What happened to the self-directed team concept?
<--- Score

142. Do you handle criticism, regardless of the situation?
<--- Score

143. What is your background in coaching and leadership and why is it important to you?
<--- Score

144. How might your organization create clear direction, alignment, and commitment for innovation?
<--- Score

145. How will you handle the situation?
<--- Score

146. Are relationships marked by trust in all directions?
<--- Score

147. How do your respective teams both support the longterm organizational strategy?

<--- Score

148. Are there situations in which you change your conflict style?
<--- Score

149. Which leadership competencies are critical for success in your organization?
<--- Score

150. Are there up-and-coming business leaders who have leadership potential?
<--- Score

151. How many field leadership days have you had since training?
<--- Score

152. How are the steps applied differently (or similarly) for each situation?
<--- Score

153. What is there about the current situation that makes it unacceptable?
<--- Score

154. What type of sales enablement leaders do you work best with?
<--- Score

155. How would you handle the situation?
<--- Score

156. Will the leadership situation strengthen?
<--- Score

157. How long did the situation last?

<--- Score

158. What would the ideal situation look like?

<--- Score

159. What involvement should the Board of Directors have?

<--- Score

160. Have you practiced coaching within your leadership team?

<--- Score

161. What are the reasons or situations that would lead to revocation of special-access privileges?

<--- Score

162. What is the situational theory of leadership?

<--- Score

163. What are the challenges that leaders face?

<--- Score

164. Why are certain leadership styles more effective in certain situations?

<--- Score

165. How does coaching differ from other forms of management practice?

<--- Score

166. Are conflict styles situational?

<--- Score

167. Is management sometimes firm, directing the

procedures must be followed?
<--- Score

168. Are you in a reinvention situation?
<--- Score

169. Does your training utilize leaders of the day ?
<--- Score

170. What are the barriers to giving your people direct access to leaders?
<--- Score

171. Does information technology lead to smaller firms?
<--- Score

172. Who are the key opposition leaders?
<--- Score

173. Will you have to share workspace, take direction from others, follow lead?
<--- Score

174. How can building your communication skills to enhance your leadership effectiveness?
<--- Score

175. How does your organization/service culture influence which domain you take a lead in?
<--- Score

176. Do you access organization support?
<--- Score

177. What is the role of the Board of Directors in

diversity and inclusion?
<--- Score

178. What is so great about directories and lead aggregators?
<--- Score

179. Is the communication relevant to the situation and to the affected population?
<--- Score

180. What ere the circumstances of the situation and how did you manage to motivate yourself?
<--- Score

181. What effect does your organizational environment have on executive coaching?
<--- Score

182. Do you take direction from others when contributing to a team project?
<--- Score

183. What is next for a sales ops leader?
<--- Score

184. What are some other situations in which listening skills are important?
<--- Score

185. What is the current situation for commodity management?
<--- Score

186. What is your style of leadership?
<--- Score

187. What are the Leadership Challenges of the Director?

<--- Score

188. Can a vision remain the same over time, despite changing leadership and educational pressures?

<--- Score

189. Does leadership believe enough of a culture of innovation and entrepreneurship exists, or can it be created?

<--- Score

190. Did the supervisor delegate to the right person?

<--- Score

191. What makes a successful coaching program?

<--- Score

192. How well did your leadership coach relate to your organization environment?

<--- Score

193. How do individuals demonstrating personal leadership act?

<--- Score

194. What was the predominant leadership approach of your former armed force?

<--- Score

195. Does organization have a dependent or lead relationship with the parties?

<--- Score

196. How might situational leadership be applied to help clarify role ambiguity?
<--- Score

197. Who are the known local sustainability leaders in business?
<--- Score

198. Did you ever wish for a do-over situation with someone?
<--- Score

199. Did he/she ever receive feedback or punitive actions for the situation(s) What was response?
<--- Score

200. Who are good leaders that you have seen or had contact with in your life?
<--- Score

201. Are competitors doing better than you are in a particular situation?
<--- Score

202. How has leadership influenced fundraising strategies?
<--- Score

203. Is the current situation supported by the available literature?
<--- Score

204. How do you meet the directive from organization leadership to reduce operational

expenses related to maintaining your network?
<--- Score

205. What can be done to help leaders overcome challenges?
<--- Score

206. How can the effectiveness of strategic leadership be enhanced?
<--- Score

207. Can anyone recommend good resources that would lead you in the right direction?
<--- Score

208. When should a leader be directive or empowering?
<--- Score

209. Are there any other situations that you would like advice on?
<--- Score

210. What principles or guidelines can be used in real-life situations?
<--- Score

211. How would you react in difficult situations?
<--- Score

212. What are some real life situations in which you have heard positive and negative feedback?
<--- Score

213. What is the relationship between your director of security and your leadership in IT?

<--- Score

214. What are the responsibilities of an interim executive director?
<--- Score

215. Are you a Servant Leader with a strong desire to be part of and lead an incredibly talented Team?
<--- Score

216. Have you established an IT strategy that clearly aligns IT with the direction of your business?
<--- Score

217. How well do the importance ratings align with your organizations strategic direction?
<--- Score

218. What is the situation from your cultural perspective?
<--- Score

219. What situations lead to unacceptable outcomes?
<--- Score

220. What role has the leading innovation project?
<--- Score

221. What type of leadership style is ideal during training?
<--- Score

222. What is the stuff of leadership?
<--- Score

223. Are you heading in the right strategic direction?

<--- Score

224. What is the boards policy if a board member is interested in the Acting, Interim or Executive Director positions?

<--- Score

225. Can a coaching leadership style help the employees to get more empowered at work?

<--- Score

226. What do you look for in a leader?

<--- Score

227. What is the boards leadership structure, and who serves as the presiding director?

<--- Score

228. How do you handle crisis situations?

<--- Score

229. Are you in a sustaining success situation?

<--- Score

230. Do you notice negative or unsettling emotions in the team and act to put the situation right?

<--- Score

231. Does the leadership team participate in forming and communicating the strategic direction?

<--- Score

232. How does an Executive Director lead a culturally competent organization?

<--- Score

233. What are some traits and characteristics of a good leader?

<--- Score

234. Are employees informed about direct contribution and benefit to meeting quality objectives?

<--- Score

235. How does your organization consultant use the first meeting effectively, to create a situation where it is possible to operate strategically, adding real business value?

<--- Score

236. What will the new situation look and feel like?

<--- Score

237. What motivates direct support staff?

<--- Score

238. Did you send directions to interview location?

<--- Score

239. What got you all going in the right direction?

<--- Score

240. Does the act team leader provide any direct services to consumers?

<--- Score

241. What administrative/leadership practices promote high quality inclusive practices and outcomes?

<--- Score

242. How have you helped others deal with a stressful situation?

<--- Score

243. What would you do differently in a similar situation?

<--- Score

244. How can adaptive leadership be applied to real-life situations?

<--- Score

245. What made them great or what are the outstanding qualities of the already stated leaders?

<--- Score

246. How do you behave and respond in a given workplace situation?

<--- Score

247. How does strategic leadership affect the determination of your organizations strategic direction?

<--- Score

248. Are your actions relative to your values dependent on the situational context?

<--- Score

249. What is it to be competent in various settings

and situations?

<--- Score

250. How do leaders choose how to direct team?

<--- Score

251. What are the characteristics of situations?

<--- Score

252. What do you know as a fact about the situation?

<--- Score

253. Does the management of your division provide strong leadership and clear strategic direction?

<--- Score

254. Does psychopathy predict desirability in dating situations?

<--- Score

255. What does collaborative leadership look like, and why does it work?

<--- Score

256. What was the stimulus in the situation, what was the response?

<--- Score

257. What do corporate directors and senior managers know about social media?

<--- Score

258. Are you in a turnaround or crisis situation?

<--- Score

259. How is your cultural self intertwined with your leadership?

<--- Score

260. Is one leadership style any better than another one in all situations?

<--- Score

261. What do you do to better prepare yourself to be an effective strategic leader?

<--- Score

262. What does autocratic leadership look like?

<--- Score

263. What are some more resources for your specific situation?

<--- Score

264. How do you know what are right actions, for oneself, in the situation?

<--- Score

265. Will the approach lead in the right direction?

<--- Score

266. How are the rest of the team handling the situation?

<--- Score

267. How much time do you give ourselves to consider difficult situations?

<--- Score

268. How do you usually respond to situations?

<--- Score

269. Have you been in a conflict situation recently?
<--- Score

270. Is your organization building managerial commitment to your organizations strategic direction?
<--- Score

271. Do you continue to be effective in building the leadership and management skills of your direct reports?
<--- Score

272. How do you create a strategic executive coaching program?
<--- Score

273. How do the leaders assemble and direct the already stated responsible for communicating the change?
<--- Score

274. What situation or when do you next want to choose to be courageous?
<--- Score

275. What actions does your executive leaders put in place to better engage with staff?
<--- Score

276. How well did you handle that situations?
<--- Score

277. Are you still moving in the right direction?

<--- Score

278. What kind of situation are you facing?
<--- Score

279. What do you do to humble yourself and direct attention to others on the team?
<--- Score

280. What is the strategic direction of your organization?
<--- Score

281. Do you pause (and seek wise counsel) periodically to set personal and group direction?
<--- Score

282. Is the new product backed by your organizations leaders and board of directors?
<--- Score

283. What relationships do you proactively strengthen to support your teams performance?
<--- Score

284. What are the different aspects of the situation?
<--- Score

285. What timelines apply to obtaining a letter of support?
<--- Score

286. How have you noticed your leadership direction being demonstrated at organization?
<--- Score

287. Why make a bad situation worse by getting all emotional?

<--- Score

288. Which organizations are the market leaders?

<--- Score

289. What situations and practices does your organization ignore that may lead to a crisis?

<--- Score

290. Are directors briefed periodically on potential liabilities?

<--- Score

291. What are team leaders main duties and role if team is self-directed?

<--- Score

292. What are the range of your roles and responsibilities as a director?

<--- Score

293. What do you do in the already stated situations?

<--- Score

294. How does the situational approach work?

<--- Score

295. How do you tend to behave in a group situation (quiet, leader)?

<--- Score

296. Is there clear strategic leadership and

direction?

<--- Score

297. How have you resolved difficult situations in the past by taking on a leadership role?

<--- Score

298. What can commercial leaders do to help?

<--- Score

299. Is the situation any better now?

<--- Score

300. Did you do different things in parallel situations?

<--- Score

301. How does transition leadership coaching work?

<--- Score

302. Why practice ethical leadership?

<--- Score

303. Why is parliamentary procedure helpful in situations?

<--- Score

304. When might brainstorming skills be helpful in a leadership situation?

<--- Score

305. Does your training have a situational leadership component?

<--- Score

306. What are the expectations on the leadership?
<--- Score

307. How will you communicate the situation?
<--- Score

308. Are all areas clear on your organizations direction?
<--- Score

309. When does charisma matter for top-level leaders?
<--- Score

310. What human limitations may have been present during the situation?
<--- Score

311. What are the key economic trends that could affect your nature or direction?
<--- Score

312. Is there mutual respect among the players and coaching staff?
<--- Score

313. What kind of financial aid is available just for employees in your situation?
<--- Score

314. Does the employee have difficulty following multiple step directions?
<--- Score

315. Is it possible for a leader to be both directive and supportive at the same time?

<--- Score

316. What are the situations in which executives leave nonprofits?
<--- Score

317. What are the qualities of good leaders?
<--- Score

318. What values should the new director demonstrate and promote?
<--- Score

319. When will you be faced with brainstorming situations in the future?
<--- Score

320. Who are the key members of your leader network?
<--- Score

321. What is your take on transactional leadership?
<--- Score

322. How are you building new leaders through situational leadership?
<--- Score

323. Is there something unique about the way one directs?
<--- Score

324. Are the facts of the situation clear, or are just observations and opinions?
<--- Score

325. How important are leadership and cultural behaviours in supporting your organizations culture of innovation?

<--- Score

326. Who is eligible for leadership coaching?

<--- Score

327. How would you suggest handling the situation with Innocent?

<--- Score

328. How does the Executive Director lead the way to having a shared organizational vision?

<--- Score

329. Do leadership actions dramatically demonstrate commitment to change?

<--- Score

330. Are senior managers directly involved in sponsoring the change?

<--- Score

331. Which leadership style should you choose?

<--- Score

332. How can digital directors add value?

<--- Score

333. Do certain situations of labour market stress encourage a more integrated approach?

<--- Score

334. Which organizations are price leaders?

<--- Score

335. Is that situation bound to remain unchanged indefinitely?
<--- Score

336. What was the situation, and what leads you to your conclusion?
<--- Score

337. What forces will tend to lead your organization to market the product through channel intermediaries rather than directly?
<--- Score

338. How do you give direction without giving directives?
<--- Score

339. Will the approach lead in a direction towards success?
<--- Score

340. What area(s) do you believe is a key strength of your leadership coach?
<--- Score

341. What does your organization do to collect contact information from leads?
<--- Score

342. Did you have to think of some specific situation to make a true difference in your language style?
<--- Score

343. What is your organizations strategic direction?

<--- Score

344. How did you cope and/or move on from the situation?

<--- Score

345. What are the perceptions of employees towards organization directors leadership styles?

<--- Score

346. How has the coaching affected your professional role and leadership style?

<--- Score

347. Is it leading in the right direction?

<--- Score

348. Are too many positions reporting to the Executive Director?

<--- Score

349. What is your organizations philosophy and practice in terms of filling key vacancies as an executive director?

<--- Score

350. What did the leader do which indicated either appropriate use or abuse?

<--- Score

351. Do you have right type of leaders leading to right direction?

<--- Score

352. Why do you call yourself Leadership Coaches?
<--- Score

353. Why is communication so important in conflict and controversy situations?
<--- Score

354. What are some leadership situations that might call for servant leadership?
<--- Score

355. What extraordinary leader has positively and directly affected your life?
<--- Score

356. What difference has it made to the local situation?
<--- Score

357. What leadership, mentoring and/or coaching roles are there?
<--- Score

358. Do you have the support of your leadership?
<--- Score

359. Have you changed staff directors recently?
<--- Score

360. Is the it leadership team directly involved in communicating the strategy?
<--- Score

361. How do you articulate a clear sense of direction and purpose?
<--- Score

362. How is the approved provider supporting the educational leader?

<--- Score

363. Does the management of your department provide strong leadership and clear strategic direction?

<--- Score

364. Is leadership in the eye of the beholder?

<--- Score

365. What is the role of a leader in a situation that is essentially collaborative and based on a principle of equity between the key players?

<--- Score

366. How do you look at your own leadership skills and leadership style?

<--- Score

367. How stressful do situations make you feel at work?

<--- Score

368. How do you deal with a person who uses a conflict management style detrimental to the situation?

<--- Score

369. Why is effective listening by all parties important in managing conflict situations?

<--- Score

370. Can majority of work be directly tied to

business strategy?

<--- Score

371. Is there clear direction from the top with clear support for getting value for money or best value in procurement?

<--- Score

372. How does your style of leadership contribute to the effectiveness of your service?

<--- Score

373. What do you believe to be essential to leadership behaviour?

<--- Score

374. How can situational leadership be successful?

<--- Score

375. Why is directive leadership the dominant leadership style in the startup phase?

<--- Score

376. Do you imagine seeing the term PM Office Office in your organization directory?

<--- Score

377. How do you adjust your leader deployment strategies to pair leaders with complementary skills sets?

<--- Score

378. What do you do to become a better leader?

<--- Score

379. How do you handle tough situations as a

technology leader?

<--- Score

380. Has a leadership succession strategy been created and sustained?

<--- Score

381. What should the board of directors/trustees and senior executives be doing?

<--- Score

382. How do visionary, situational, and transforming leadership models contribute to effective servant leadership?

<--- Score

383. What do you feel about the current situation/ conflict/tension/uncertainty?

<--- Score

384. How would situations turn out differently if you were slower to make judgments?

<--- Score

385. What is in it for Business Leaders?

<--- Score

386. How do you approach the situation from a new and broader perspective?

<--- Score

387. Where should the shared-services organization be situated?

<--- Score

388. Did the situation change with new releases/

versions?

<--- Score

389. How does the leadership view the role of technology in your organization?

<--- Score

390. How do you let go of the existing situation and move on to something new?

<--- Score

391. Are the board members paid to serve on the board of directors?

<--- Score

392. Does the leadership maintain a consistent approach and direction?

<--- Score

393. Is coaching an evolved form of leadership?

<--- Score

394. What are the communication expectations in emergency situations?

<--- Score

395. What reward can a leader offer to motivate workforce?

<--- Score

396. What positive qualities (as attitudes, virtues, or principles) do you possess as a leader?

<--- Score

397. Is your board effective in giving direction?

<--- Score

398. What are self-directed work teams?
<--- Score

399. Why might situational leadership be considered the best style?
<--- Score

400. When should an Executive Director lead, manage, or support others?
<--- Score

401. How are minority laborers networked with minority leaders?
<--- Score

402. How much information should subordinates receive about your organizations strategic direction?
<--- Score

403. What would actions be in similar situations?
<--- Score

404. What is the simplest, surest, and most direct way of getting someone to do something?
<--- Score

405. How capable is IT in supporting the mission of the business?
<--- Score

406. Does effective leadership vary with different situations?
<--- Score

407. What is the most appropriate leadership style according to different types of situations?
<--- Score

408. Who do you know who has encountered a similar situation?
<--- Score

409. How often should meetings occur, time, future direction?
<--- Score

410. How do you want the Executive Director/ Board relationship to change?
<--- Score

411. How do you exercise interpersonal power as a leader?
<--- Score

412. Do you give your organization direction?
<--- Score

413. Are you offering enough for the middle organization athletic directors?
<--- Score

414. Is there one best method or leadership style to be used by a coach?
<--- Score

415. How can leaders overcome cultural biases?
<--- Score

416. Why is there special emphasis on sales leadership?

<--- Score

417. What are your triggers (people and situations most likely to trigger negative or uncomfortable emotions)?
<--- Score

418. Can the situation be seen from a different perspective?
<--- Score

419. What if someone on the team won fit follow your directions?
<--- Score

420. Does effective charismatic leadership depend on the situation?
<--- Score

421. Is your organization project leader ensuring that testing is performed and that the most appropriate testing program is applied to the situation?
<--- Score

422. What exactly does a sales enablement leader do?
<--- Score

423. Does the vision promote change and a sense of direction?
<--- Score

424. Are you leading with your brand direction?
<--- Score

425. How do you apply for the Leadership Coaching program?
<--- Score

426. Will leadership be changed or stay the same?
<--- Score

427. How do managers pursue leadership in conflicts when facing notice of dismissal?
<--- Score

428. Where was the Board of Directors?
<--- Score

429. What is the competitor situation?
<--- Score

430. What is one thing that you see as different between your (individual contributor) product manager role and product leader roles with formal direct reports?
<--- Score

431. What does situational leadership primarily help followers do?
<--- Score

432. Does the leadership situation strengthen?
<--- Score

433. Why did coaching vary so much even in organizations where coaches carried the same workload?
<--- Score

434. What factors in a given situation are leading

you to think of someone as a suspect?

<--- Score

435. Are you coaching and training your new Leaders?

<--- Score

436. Is the program director or organization representative an officer on the board of directors?

<--- Score

437. How are ethics-related behaviors modeled by organizational leaders?

<--- Score

438. How will the strategic-leader environment change in the future?

<--- Score

439. What are situations in which you will have to participate in a behavioral interview?

<--- Score

440. What competencies should directors possess?

<--- Score

441. What office space is available for the director that will be accessible, convenient and allows for a certain amount of privacy?

<--- Score

442. What is your organizations direction for communication?

<--- Score

443. Does your organization have directors and

officers liability coverage?

<--- Score

444. How do you exercise organizational power as a leader?

<--- Score

445. Do you intend to participate on the board of directors?

<--- Score

446. How comfortable or uncomfortable did you feel in the interview situation?

<--- Score

447. Are you in a start-up situation?

<--- Score

448. What is your leadership vision for the future direction of your organization?

<--- Score

449. What strategic goals does your organization have to achieve, and how can coaching support the already stated?

<--- Score

450. What do you know about the current situation?

<--- Score

451. How do you incorporate visionary, situational, and transforming leadership models in your leadership roles?

<--- Score

452. What is the distribution future mobile, internet, physical or direct sales?
<--- Score

453. How do you lead by supporting the leadership of others?
<--- Score

454. What key indicators help the leadership team assess performance?
<--- Score

455. Do you have everyone/everything working in the same direction?
<--- Score

456. How long will it be before the situation returns to normal?
<--- Score

457. What is unarguable about the situation?
<--- Score

458. How are you supporting leadership engagement?
<--- Score

459. Do you know who to call and where to go under a life-threatening situation?
<--- Score

460. When is it appropriate to employ each strategic leadership style?
<--- Score

461. How do you build workable relationships with

the principals and leadership teams?
<--- Score

462. Do you have an overarching tool that keeps everything moving in the same direction?
<--- Score

463. How do you begin to incorporate servant leadership qualities into your work as an executive director?
<--- Score

464. How do you become better leaders of your organization?
<--- Score

465. What is the ratio of leadership to direct reports?
<--- Score

466. Which quadrant of the situational leadership style did one apply?
<--- Score

467. Are you confident that your leaders know how to create a sense of purpose and direction?
<--- Score

468. Which failures in information protection is most likely to directly lead to your organization losing its ability to continue as a going concern?
<--- Score

469. Where there situations today when you should have spent more time listening instead of solving?

<--- Score

470. How do you manage the situation?
<--- Score

471. What made the situation difficult?
<--- Score

472. What style of leadership is most effective in a particular situation with a specific group of followers?
<--- Score

473. Does the asset have value assigned directly by your organization?
<--- Score

474. How should the departing director relate to your organization after the transition?
<--- Score

475. Are there situations when neither an employee-oriented or structured leader is indicated?
<--- Score

476. How will you remind yourself of the new behaviors in similar situations?
<--- Score

477. Is capital shifting in the right direction?
<--- Score

478. Does doing good always lead to doing better?
<--- Score

479. How accurate is your situational awareness & why?

<--- Score

480. What is the current financial situation of your business?

<--- Score

481. Have you had any other leadership position where notice of dismissal was a part of your work?

<--- Score

482. How are the participants coping with the situation?

<--- Score

483. Do you offer direct access for your people to connect with leaders?

<--- Score

484. Are your leaders sensitive to each current situation?

<--- Score

485. Do you differ the concepts leader and manager?

<--- Score

486. What are the supports and rewards of being a director?

<--- Score

487. What style of leadership helps organizations thrive in crisis situations?

<--- Score

488. What was the situation, what did you do, and what was the outcome?

<--- Score

489. Does good situational awareness always lead to good performance?

<--- Score

490. Which leadership style works best for various situations in the field?

<--- Score

491. Is there no allowance the collective leadership can forego that would help the situation or at least communicate compassion?

<--- Score

492. Do ones actions vary depending on the situation?

<--- Score

493. What is the leadership in a particular situation for?

<--- Score

494. How willing are members of your organization to accept leadership and direction from management?

<--- Score

495. Where do you add value directly to the customer experience versus indirectly through employees?

<--- Score

496. What are the factors of situational leadership?

<--- Score

497. What are the skills and traits of sales enablement leaders?
<--- Score

498. Does your organization have a TQM Director, Consultant or other position responsible for implementation of the principles of TQM?
<--- Score

499. What are the key challenges leaders will face based on current strategy and direction?
<--- Score

500. How will you maintain a phone directory covering all sites?
<--- Score

501. What role do senior leaders play in agreeing upon and implementing tactical objectives?
<--- Score

502. How do you articulate a clear sense of direction and purpose for your organization?
<--- Score

503. Do you provide direction and a sense of meaning to others by reminding them of what is important?
<--- Score

504. Do leaders, managers and employees have sufficient organizational change capabilities to manage change challenges by tailoring common methods and tools to specific situations?

<--- Score

505. When will you be faced with an interview situation?
<--- Score

506. Do you apply the same leadership style as your previous superior?
<--- Score

507. Does your organization have an exit that leads directly to the outside?
<--- Score

508. What are the situations in which each of leaders find themselves?
<--- Score

509. Is it time for some fresh, new Directors, with different messages?
<--- Score

510. What do you hope to gain from Leadership Coaching?
<--- Score

511. Why did the already stated leader(s) shout out directions?
<--- Score

512. What is the secret of the leaders who are aligned, funded, and confident of ability to affect strategic business goals directly?
<--- Score

513. What direction will the movement take?

<--- Score

514. What were the Executive Directors performance highlights in the past year?
<--- Score

515. What is the long-term direction of your organization?
<--- Score

516. What happens when leaders emotions cannot be logically anticipated based on the situation?
<--- Score

517. How has your leadership evolved since you started coaching?
<--- Score

518. What direction are you moving in?
<--- Score

519. What is any prior work of yours relevant to leading and directing new and expanding roles and responsibilities, and how you managed expectations within your organization?
<--- Score

520. Is it relevant to your situation?
<--- Score

521. What is your level of influence and direct authority?
<--- Score

522. What better way to guarantee lead quality and increase lead values than having committed

users calling service providers directly?

<--- Score

523. How have you demonstrated leadership skills within a group situation?

<--- Score

524. Are there situations when it is necessary?

<--- Score

525. How do the leadership styles directly affect staff motivation?

<--- Score

526. Does it depend on the situation?

<--- Score

527. Where to next for educational leadership?

<--- Score

528. Have you ever been in a situation where it would be a lot easier to compromise?

<--- Score

529. How long has your organization been involved directly in implementation of TQM?

<--- Score

530. What specific actions are you taking now to be more effective in your leadership situation on a personal, group, and systems level?

<--- Score

531. Are you doing the right thing in the situation?

<--- Score

532. Is online leadership training effective?

<--- Score

533. How well does your leadership training program prepare current and future managers and supervisors?

<--- Score

534. Is best buy leadership supporting efforts to have other departments use the mam?

<--- Score

Add up total points for this section:
_ _ _ _ _ = Total points for this section

Divided by: _ _ _ _ _ _ (number of statements answered) = _ _ _ _ _ _
Average score for this section

Transfer your score to the Situational Leadership Index at the beginning of the Self-Assessment.

Situational Leadership and Managing Projects, Criteria for Project Managers:

1.0 Initiating Process Group: Situational Leadership

1. Were decisions made in a timely manner?

2. Does it make any difference if you am successful?

3. What will you do to minimize the impact should a risk event occur?

4. Establishment of pm office?

5. Realistic - are the desired results expressed in a way that the team will be motivated and believe that the required level of involvement will be obtained?

6. Who are the Situational Leadership project stakeholders?

7. Measurable - are the targets measurable?

8. First of all, should any action be taken?

9. Do you know if the Situational Leadership project requires outside equipment or vendor resources?

10. Do you know all the stakeholders impacted by the Situational Leadership project and what needs are?

11. Professionals want to know what is expected from them what are the deliverables?

12. Are you properly tracking the progress of the Situational Leadership project and communicating the status to stakeholders?

13. Are you certain deliverables are properly completed and meet quality standards?

14. Did the Situational Leadership project team have the right skills?

15. Do you know the Situational Leadership projects goal, purpose and objectives?

16. Do you understand the quality and control criteria that must be achieved for successful Situational Leadership project completion?

17. Did you use a contractor or vendor?

18. What are the constraints?

19. In which Situational Leadership project management process group is the detailed Situational Leadership project budget created?

20. How should needs be met?

1.1 Project Charter: Situational Leadership

21. How high should you set your goals?

22. Situational Leadership project objective statement: what must the Situational Leadership project do?

23. Why the improvements?

24. Are you building in-house ?

25. Avoid costs, improve service, and/ or comply with a mandate?

26. What does it need to do?

27. Who are the stakeholders?

28. What is the justification?

29. Customer: who are you doing the Situational Leadership project for?

30. Is it an improvement over existing products?

31. What are the assumptions?

32. How will you know a change is an improvement?

33. Situational Leadership project background: what is the primary motivation for this Situational Leadership

project?

34. Situational Leadership project deliverables: what is the Situational Leadership project going to produce?

35. Are there special technology requirements?

36. Run it as as a startup?

37. Pop quiz – which are the same inputs as in the Situational Leadership project charter?

38. Where and how does the team fit within your organization structure?

39. Market – identify products market, including whether it is outside of the objective: what is the purpose of the program or Situational Leadership project?

40. Assumptions: what factors, for planning purposes, are you considering to be true?

1.2 Stakeholder Register: Situational Leadership

41. How big is the gap?

42. What is the power of the stakeholder?

43. What & Why?

44. Who is managing stakeholder engagement?

45. How should employers make voices heard?

46. Is your organization ready for change?

47. What opportunities exist to provide communications?

48. What are the major Situational Leadership project milestones requiring communications or providing communications opportunities?

49. Who wants to talk about Security?

50. How will reports be created?

51. How much influence do they have on the Situational Leadership project?

1.3 Stakeholder Analysis Matrix: Situational Leadership

52. Beneficiaries; who are the potential beneficiaries?

53. Who will obstruct/hinder the Situational Leadership project if they are not involved?

54. How to measure the achievement of the Outputs?

55. What can the Situational Leadership projects outcome be used for?

56. Political effects?

57. Who holds positions of responsibility in interested organizations?

58. What mechanisms are proposed to monitor and measure Situational Leadership project performance in terms of social development outcomes?

59. Lack of competitive strength?

60. What should thwe organizations stakeholders avoid?

61. Industry or lifestyle trends?

62. Innovative aspects?

63. Could any of your organizations weaknesses seriously threaten development?

64. What resources might the stakeholder bring to the Situational Leadership project?

65. What do you Evaluate?

66. Why involve the stakeholder?

67. Does the stakeholder want to be involved or merely need to be informed about the Situational Leadership project and its process?

68. Accreditations, etc?

69. Economy - home, abroad?

70. Experience, knowledge, data?

71. Vulnerable groups; who are the vulnerable groups that might be affected by the Situational Leadership project?

2.0 Planning Process Group: Situational Leadership

72. Do the partners have sufficient financial capacity to keep up the benefits produced by the programme?

73. What is the NEXT thing to do?

74. In what way has the Situational Leadership project come up with innovative measures for problem-solving?

75. Who are the Situational Leadership project stakeholders?

76. The Situational Leadership project charter is created in which Situational Leadership project management process group?

77. Why do it Situational Leadership projects fail?

78. To what extent do the intervention objectives and strategies of the Situational Leadership project respond to your organizations plans?

79. Just how important is your work to the overall success of the Situational Leadership project?

80. What is the critical path for this Situational Leadership project, and what is the duration of the critical path?

81. Are work methodologies, financial instruments,

etc. shared among departments, organizations and Situational Leadership projects?

82. In which Situational Leadership project management process group is the detailed Situational Leadership project budget created?

83. What factors are contributing to progress or delay in the achievement of products and results?

84. To what extent has the intervention strategy been adapted to the areas of intervention in which it is being implemented?

85. If a risk event occurs, what will you do?

86. Have more efficient (sensitive) and appropriate measures been adopted to respond to the political and socio-cultural problems identified?

87. Will you be replaced?

88. What is a Software Development Life Cycle (SDLC)?

89. What type of estimation method are you using?

90. How will you know you did it?

2.1 Project Management Plan: Situational Leadership

91. Development trends and opportunities. What if the positive direction and vision of your organization causes expected trends to change?

92. What happened during the process that you found interesting?

93. What are the training needs?

94. When is the Situational Leadership project management plan created?

95. Who manages integration?

96. Are calculations and results of analyzes essentially correct?

97. What does management expect of PMs?

98. Are there any client staffing expectations?

99. If the Situational Leadership project is complex or scope is specialized, do you have appropriate and/or qualified staff available to perform the tasks?

100. What worked well?

101. Is the budget realistic?

102. What is risk management?

103. What would you do differently what did not work?

104. What is the business need?

105. What should you drop in order to add something new?

106. What went wrong?

107. Are there any scope changes proposed for a previously authorized Situational Leadership project?

108. What are the deliverables?

109. What did not work so well?

2.2 Scope Management Plan: Situational Leadership

110. What happens if scope changes?

111. What is the estimated cost of creating and implementing?

112. Are the appropriate IT resources adequate to meet planned commitments?

113. Does the business case include how the Situational Leadership project aligns with your organizations strategic goals & objectives?

114. How do you know when you are finished?

115. Are tasks tracked by hours?

116. Have the personnel with the necessary skills and competence been identified and has agreement for participation in the Situational Leadership project been reached with the appropriate management?

117. Are Situational Leadership project team members committed fulltime?

118. Is there a formal process for updating the Situational Leadership project baseline?

119. Is there a formal set of procedures supporting Issues Management?

120. Have activity relationships and interdependencies within tasks been adequately identified?

121. What is the most common tool for helping define the detail?

122. Can each item be appropriately scheduled?

123. Has adequate time for orientation & training of Situational Leadership project staff been provided for in relation to technical nature of the application and the experience levels of Situational Leadership project personnel?

124. Are corrective actions taken when actual results are substantially different from detailed Situational Leadership project plan (variances)?

125. Are written status reports provided on a designated frequent basis?

126. What does the critical path really mean?

127. Product – what are you trying to accomplish and how will you know when you are finished?

128. Are changes in scope (deliverable commitments) agreed to by all affected groups & individuals?

129. Are cause and effect determined for risks when they occur?

2.3 Requirements Management Plan: Situational Leadership

130. How will you develop the schedule of requirements activities?

131. Is stakeholder risk tolerance an important factor for the requirements process in this Situational Leadership project?

132. Did you provide clear and concise specifications?

133. What information regarding the Situational Leadership project requirements will be reported?

134. Who will finally present the work or product(s) for acceptance?

135. Which hardware or software, related to, or as outcome of the Situational Leadership project is new to your organization?

136. What performance metrics will be used?

137. Do you understand the role that each stakeholder will play in the requirements process?

138. How will you communicate scheduled tasks to other team members?

139. How will the information be distributed?

140. Did you distinguish the scope of work the

contractor(s) will be required to do?

141. Business analysis scope?

142. What went right?

143. In case of software development; Should you have a test for each code module?

144. Is the user satisfied?

145. Who will perform the analysis?

146. Who will approve the requirements (and if multiple approvers, in what order)?

147. When and how will a requirements baseline be established in this Situational Leadership project?

148. Will the contractors involved take full responsibility?

2.4 Requirements Documentation: Situational Leadership

149. How will requirements be documented and who signs off on them?

150. Can the requirement be changed without a large impact on other requirements?

151. How does what is being described meet the business need?

152. What if the system wasn t implemented?

153. Who is involved?

154. What will be the integration problems?

155. How will they be documented / shared?

156. Is the requirement properly understood?

157. The problem with gathering requirements is right there in the word gathering. What images does it conjure?

158. Basic work/business process; high-level, what is being touched?

159. What is the risk associated with cost and schedule?

160. How to document system requirements?

161. Can the requirements be checked?

162. If applicable; are there issues linked with the fact that this is an offshore Situational Leadership project?

163. Are all functions required by the customer included?

164. Is the requirement realistically testable?

165. Who is interacting with the system?

166. How linear / iterative is your Requirements Gathering process (or will it be)?

167. Validity. does the system provide the functions which best support the customers needs?

168. Is the origin of the requirement clearly stated?

2.5 Requirements Traceability Matrix: Situational Leadership

169. Will you use a Requirements Traceability Matrix?

170. What are the chronologies, contingencies, consequences, criteria?

171. Why use a WBS?

172. How small is small enough?

173. Do you have a clear understanding of all subcontracts in place?

174. Is there a requirements traceability process in place?

175. What percentage of Situational Leadership projects are producing traceability matrices between requirements and other work products?

176. What is the WBS?

177. Describe the process for approving requirements so they can be added to the traceability matrix and Situational Leadership project work can be performed. Will the Situational Leadership project requirements become approved in writing?

178. Why do you manage scope?

179. How will it affect the stakeholders personally in

career?

180. How do you manage scope?

2.6 Project Scope Statement: Situational Leadership

181. How will you verify the accuracy of the work of the Situational Leadership project, and what constitutes acceptance of the deliverables?

182. What are the major deliverables of the Situational Leadership project?

183. Any new risks introduced or old risks impacted. Are there issues that could affect the existing requirements for the result, service, or product if the scope changes?

184. Did your Situational Leadership project ask for this?

185. Are there specific processes you will use to evaluate and approve/reject changes?

186. Will there be a Change Control Process in place?

187. Have the configuration management functions been assigned?

188. Will statistics related to QA be collected, trends analyzed, and problems raised as issues?

189. What is change?

190. Have the reports to be produced, distributed, and filed been defined?

191. Situational Leadership project lead, team lead, solution architect?

192. Is there a Change Management Board?

193. Change management vs. change leadership - what is the difference?

194. Is the scope of your Situational Leadership project well defined?

195. Relevant - ask yourself can you get there; why are you doing this Situational Leadership project?

196. Is the Situational Leadership project organization documented and on file?

197. Are the input requirements from the team members clearly documented and communicated?

2.7 Assumption and Constraint Log: Situational Leadership

198. Do the requirements meet the standards of correctness, completeness, consistency, accuracy, and readability?

199. How many Situational Leadership project staff does this specific process affect?

200. Do you know what your customers expectations are regarding this process?

201. Can the requirements be traced to the appropriate components of the solution, as well as test scripts?

202. Have all involved stakeholders and work groups committed to the Situational Leadership project?

203. Are there ways to reduce the time it takes to get something approved?

204. Does the plan conform to standards?

205. Has a Situational Leadership project Communications Plan been developed?

206. Diagrams and tables are included to account for complex concepts and increase overall readability?

207. No superfluous information or marketing narrative?

208. Is the current scope of the Situational Leadership project substantially different than that originally defined in the approved Situational Leadership project plan?

209. Is there documentation of system capability requirements, data requirements, environment requirements, security requirements, and computer and hardware requirements?

210. Are there procedures in place to effectively manage interdependencies with other Situational Leadership projects / systems?

211. Have all stakeholders been identified?

212. Does the traceability documentation describe the tool and/or mechanism to be used to capture traceability throughout the life cycle?

213. Does a specific action and/or state that is known to violate security policy occur?

214. Is the amount of effort justified by the anticipated value of forming a new process?

215. Does the document/deliverable meet general requirements (for example, statement of work) for all deliverables?

216. Security analysis has access to information that is sanitized?

217. Is the process working, and people are not executing in compliance of the process?

2.8 Work Breakdown Structure: Situational Leadership

218. Is the work breakdown structure (wbs) defined and is the scope of the Situational Leadership project clear with assigned deliverable owners?

219. How many levels?

220. When do you stop?

221. Where does it take place?

222. When would you develop a Work Breakdown Structure?

223. Is it a change in scope?

224. Is it still viable?

225. Why would you develop a Work Breakdown Structure?

226. What is the probability that the Situational Leadership project duration will exceed xx weeks?

227. How big is a work-package?

228. What is the probability of completing the Situational Leadership project in less that xx days?

229. How will you and your Situational Leadership project team define the Situational Leadership

projects scope and work breakdown structure?

230. How much detail?

231. How far down?

232. What has to be done?

233. Do you need another level?

234. Can you make it?

235. Who has to do it?

2.9 WBS Dictionary: Situational Leadership

236. Are the responsibilities and authorities of each of the above organizational elements or managers clearly defined?

237. The Situational Leadership projected business base for each period?

238. Are all affected work authorizations, budgeting, and scheduling documents amended to properly reflect the effects of authorized changes?

239. Contemplated overhead expenditure for each period based on the best information currently available?

240. Are work packages reasonably short in time duration or do they have adequate objective indicators/milestones to minimize subjectivity of the in process work evaluation?

241. Are overhead costs budgets established on a basis consistent with anticipated direct business base?

242. Are records maintained to show full accountability for all material purchased for the contract, including the residual inventory?

243. What is the end result of a work package?

244. Where learning is used in developing underlying budgets is there a direct relationship between anticipated learning and time phased budgets?

245. Are estimates developed by Situational Leadership project personnel coordinated with the already stated responsible for overall management to determine whether required resources will be available according to revised planning?

246. Does the contractors system description or procedures require that the performance measurement baseline plus management reserve equal the contract budget base?

247. Are significant decision points, constraints, and interfaces identified as key milestones?

248. Are the requirements for all items of overhead established by rational, traceable processes?

249. Are Situational Leadership projected overhead costs in each pool and the associated direct costs used as the basis for establishing interim rates for allocating overhead to contracts?

250. Budgeted cost for work performed?

251. Are indirect costs accumulated for comparison with the corresponding budgets?

252. What size should a work package be?

253. Does the scheduling system provide for the identification of work progress against technical and other milestones, and also provide for forecasts of

completion dates of scheduled work?

254. Are the variances between budgeted and actual indirect costs identified and analyzed at the level of assigned responsibility for control (indirect pool, department, etc.)?

255. Are data being used by managers in an effective manner to ascertain Situational Leadership project or functional status, to identify reasons or significant variance, and to initiate appropriate corrective action?

2.10 Schedule Management Plan: Situational Leadership

256. Has the schedule been baselined?

257. Has a quality assurance plan been developed for the Situational Leadership project?

258. Are the people assigned to the Situational Leadership project sufficiently qualified?

259. Are all key components of a Quality Assurance Plan present?

260. Is the critical path valid?

261. Are the Situational Leadership project team members located locally to the users/stakeholders?

262. Is the correct WBS element identified for each task and milestone in the IMS?

263. Time for overtime?

264. Situational Leadership project definition & scope?

265. Are the schedule estimates reasonable given the Situational Leadership project?

266. Are corrective actions and variances reported?

267. Have the key functions and capabilities been

defined and assigned to each release or iteration?

268. Is there any form of automated support for Issues Management?

269. Has the Situational Leadership project manager been identified?

270. Staffing Requirements?

271. Is there a set of procedures defining the scope, procedures, and deliverables defining quality control?

272. What is the difference between % Complete and % work?

273. Is there an onboarding process in place?

274. What is the estimated time to complete the Situational Leadership project if status quo is maintained?

2.11 Activity List: Situational Leadership

275. What did not go as well?

276. Are the required resources available or need to be acquired?

277. What is the LF and LS for each activity?

278. How detailed should a Situational Leadership project get?

279. When will the work be performed?

280. In what sequence?

281. Is there anything planned that does not need to be here?

282. How difficult will it be to do specific activities on this Situational Leadership project?

283. How do you determine the late start (LS) for each activity?

284. Should you include sub-activities?

285. Who will perform the work?

286. For other activities, how much delay can be tolerated?

287. When do the individual activities need to start and finish?

288. How can the Situational Leadership project be displayed graphically to better visualize the activities?

289. What is the total time required to complete the Situational Leadership project if no delays occur?

290. How much slack is available in the Situational Leadership project?

291. What are you counting on?

292. How should ongoing costs be monitored to try to keep the Situational Leadership project within budget?

293. Where will it be performed?

2.12 Activity Attributes: Situational Leadership

294. Have constraints been applied to the start and finish milestones for the phases?

295. Does your organization of the data change its meaning?

296. How else could the items be grouped?

297. Which method produces the more accurate cost assignment?

298. Activity: what is Missing?

299. Resources to accomplish the work?

300. How much activity detail is required?

301. How many resources do you need to complete the work scope within a limit of X number of days?

302. Why?

303. Do you feel very comfortable with your prediction?

304. How difficult will it be to complete specific activities on this Situational Leadership project?

305. Where else does it apply?

306. What is your organizations history in doing similar activities?

307. What conclusions/generalizations can you draw from this?

308. Has management defined a definite timeframe for the turnaround or Situational Leadership project window?

309. What is missing?

2.13 Milestone List: Situational Leadership

310. Calculate how long can activity be delayed?

311. What specific improvements did you make to the Situational Leadership project proposal since the previous time?

312. Effects on core activities, distraction?

313. Describe the concept of the technology, product or service that will be or has been developed. How will it be used?

314. How will the milestone be verified?

315. Milestone pages should display the UserID of the person who added the milestone. Does a report or query exist that provides this audit information?

316. What has been done so far?

317. What are your competitors vulnerabilities?

318. Sustainable financial backing?

319. It is to be a narrative text providing the crucial aspects of your Situational Leadership project proposal answering what, who, how, when and where?

320. Global influences?

321. How soon can the activity finish?

322. Loss of key staff?

323. How late can the activity finish?

324. Describe the industry you are in and the market growth opportunities. What is the market for your technology, product or service?

325. What background experience, skills, and strengths does the team bring to your organization?

326. Usps (unique selling points)?

327. Can you derive how soon can the whole Situational Leadership project finish?

328. Gaps in capabilities?

2.14 Network Diagram: Situational Leadership

329. What must be completed before an activity can be started?

330. How difficult will it be to do specific activities on this Situational Leadership project?

331. Planning: who, how long, what to do?

332. If x is long, what would be the completion time if you break x into two parallel parts of y weeks and z weeks?

333. Are the required resources available?

334. What activities must occur simultaneously with this activity?

335. If the Situational Leadership project network diagram cannot change and you have extra personnel resources, what is the BEST thing to do?

336. If a current contract exists, can you provide the vendor name, contract start, and contract expiration date?

337. What activity must be completed immediately before this activity can start?

338. What are the Major Administrative Issues?

339. What job or jobs could run concurrently?

340. What is the completion time?

341. What job or jobs follow it?

342. Where do schedules come from?

343. Can you calculate the confidence level?

344. Why must you schedule milestones, such as reviews, throughout the Situational Leadership project?

345. What controls the start and finish of a job?

346. Which type of network diagram allows you to depict four types of dependencies?

2.15 Activity Resource Requirements: Situational Leadership

347. How do you manage time?

348. Are there unresolved issues that need to be addressed?

349. Why do you do that?

350. What is the Work Plan Standard?

351. Other support in specific areas?

352. Organizational Applicability?

353. How many signatures do you require on a check and does this match what is in your policy and procedures?

354. Do you use tools like decomposition and rolling-wave planning to produce the activity list and other outputs?

355. How do you handle petty cash?

356. When does monitoring begin?

357. Anything else?

358. What are constraints that you might find during the Human Resource Planning process?

359. Which logical relationship does the PDM use most often?

2.16 Resource Breakdown Structure: Situational Leadership

360. What is Situational Leadership project communication management?

361. Which resources should be in the resource pool?

362. How difficult will it be to do specific activities on this Situational Leadership project?

363. The list could probably go on, but, the thing that you would most like to know is, How long & How much?

364. Who needs what information?

365. Why is this important?

366. Who is allowed to see what data about which resources?

367. Why time management?

368. What defines a successful Situational Leadership project?

369. Goals for the Situational Leadership project. What is each stakeholders desired outcome for the Situational Leadership project?

370. Who is allowed to perform which functions?

371. What are the requirements for resource data?

372. Which resource planning tool provides information on resource responsibility and accountability?

373. Why do you do it?

374. What defines a successful Situational Leadership project?

375. How can this help you with team building?

2.17 Activity Duration Estimates: Situational Leadership

376. What is the BEST thing to do?

377. Does the case present a realistic scenario?

378. Account for the make-or-buy process and how to perform the financial calculations involved in the process. What are the main types of contracts if you do decide to outsource?

379. What does it mean to take a systems view of a Situational Leadership project?

380. What is wrong with this scenario?

381. Describe Situational Leadership project integration management in your own words. How does Situational Leadership project integration management relate to the Situational Leadership project life cycle, stakeholders, and the other Situational Leadership project management knowledge areas?

382. What are key inputs and outputs of the software?

383. How is the Situational Leadership project doing?

384. Which best describes how this affects the Situational Leadership project?

385. Are steps identified by which Situational

Leadership project documents may be changed?

386. What is the difference between conceptual, application, and evaluative questions?

387. What functions does this software provide that cannot be done easily using other tools such as a spreadsheet or database?

388. After changes are approved are Situational Leadership project documents updated and distributed?

389. Why is it difficult to use Situational Leadership project management software well?

390. What are the three main outputs of quality control?

391. Are activity duration estimates documented?

392. Do stakeholders follow a procedure for formally accepting the Situational Leadership project scope?

393. How do theories relate to Situational Leadership project management?

394. Are Situational Leadership project management tools and techniques consistently applied throughout all Situational Leadership projects?

395. What are the Situational Leadership project management deliverables of each process group?

2.18 Duration Estimating Worksheet: Situational Leadership

396. When does your organization expect to be able to complete it?

397. Done before proceeding with this activity or what can be done concurrently?

398. Do any colleagues have experience with your organization and/or RFPs?

399. Small or large Situational Leadership project?

400. Can the Situational Leadership project be constructed as planned?

401. Science = process: remember the scientific method?

402. What is your role?

403. What utility impacts are there?

404. Why estimate costs?

405. What is cost and Situational Leadership project cost management?

406. When, then?

407. Value pocket identification & quantification what are value pockets?

408. What info is needed?

409. How can the Situational Leadership project be displayed graphically to better visualize the activities?

410. What work will be included in the Situational Leadership project?

411. What questions do you have?

412. What are the critical bottleneck activities?

2.19 Project Schedule: Situational Leadership

413. How can you fix it?

414. If there are any qualifying green components to this Situational Leadership project, what portion of the total Situational Leadership project cost is green?

415. Was the Situational Leadership project schedule reviewed by all stakeholders and formally accepted?

416. Your best shot for providing estimations how complex/how much work does the activity require?

417. The wbs is developed as part of a joint planning session. and how do you know that youhave done this right?

418. Are there activities that came from a template or previous Situational Leadership project that are not applicable on this phase of this Situational Leadership project?

419. How detailed should a Situational Leadership project get?

420. What documents, if any, will the subcontractor provide (eg Situational Leadership project schedule, quality plan etc)?

421. Your Situational Leadership project management plan results in a Situational Leadership project

schedule that is too long. If the Situational Leadership project network diagram cannot change and you have extra personnel resources, what is the BEST thing to do?

422. It allows the Situational Leadership project to be delivered on schedule. How Do you Use Schedules?

423. What is the most mis-scheduled part of process?

424. If you can not fix it, how do you do it differently?

425. How can slack be negative?

426. Did the Situational Leadership project come in under budget?

427. Why is this particularly bad?

428. Is infrastructure setup part of your Situational Leadership project?

429. Should you have a test for each code module?

430. What is risk?

2.20 Cost Management Plan: Situational Leadership

431. Has a provision been made to reassess Situational Leadership project risks at various Situational Leadership project stages?

432. Is documentation created for communication with the suppliers and Vendors?

433. Has the Situational Leadership project scope been baselined?

434. What are the Situational Leadership project objectives?

435. Are action items captured and managed?

436. Is the communication plan being followed?

437. Have all documents been archived in a Situational Leadership project repository for each release?

438. Is your organization certified as a supplier, wholesaler, regular dealer, or manufacturer of corresponding products/supplies?

439. Does a documented Situational Leadership project organizational policy & plan (i.e. governance model) exist?

440. Have all team members been part of identifying

risks?

441. Forecasts – how will the cost to complete the Situational Leadership project be forecast?

442. Is there anything unique in this Situational Leadership projects scope statement that will affect resources?

443. Similar Situational Leadership projects?

444. Are schedule deliverables actually delivered?

445. What is cost and Situational Leadership project cost management?

446. For cost control purposes?

447. Are parking lot items captured?

448. Is stakeholder involvement adequate?

449. Are vendor contract reports, reviews and visits conducted periodically?

2.21 Activity Cost Estimates: Situational Leadership

450. Was it performed on time?

451. Were the costs or charges reasonable?

452. Based on your Situational Leadership project communication management plan, what worked well?

453. How Award?

454. Is costing method consistent with study goals?

455. Does the estimator have experience?

456. Was the consultant knowledgeable about the program?

457. How do you fund change orders?

458. What makes a good expected result statement?

459. Does the activity serve a common type of customer?

460. Did the consultant work with local staff to develop local capacity?

461. Where can you get activity reports?

462. What is the activity inventory?

463. Which contract type places the most risk on the seller?

464. How quickly can the task be done with the skills available?

465. Are data needed on characteristics of care?

466. Will you use any tools, such as Situational Leadership project management software, to assist in capturing Earned Value metrics?

467. How do you allocate indirect costs to activities?

2.22 Cost Estimating Worksheet: Situational Leadership

468. Does the Situational Leadership project provide innovative ways for stakeholders to overcome obstacles or deliver better outcomes?

469. How will the results be shared and to whom?

470. Who is best positioned to know and assist in identifying corresponding factors?

471. Ask: are others positioned to know, are others credible, and will others cooperate?

472. Identify the timeframe necessary to monitor progress and collect data to determine how the selected measure has changed?

473. Is it feasible to establish a control group arrangement?

474. What costs are to be estimated?

475. What is the purpose of estimating?

476. What happens to any remaining funds not used?

477. Can a trend be established from historical performance data on the selected measure and are the criteria for using trend analysis or forecasting methods met?

478. Is the Situational Leadership project responsive to community need?

479. What is the estimated labor cost today based upon this information?

480. What additional Situational Leadership project(s) could be initiated as a result of this Situational Leadership project?

481. What will others want?

482. What can be included?

483. Will the Situational Leadership project collaborate with the local community and leverage resources?

2.23 Cost Baseline: Situational Leadership

484. Have the resources used by the Situational Leadership project been reassigned to other units or Situational Leadership projects?

485. Are procedures defined by which the cost baseline may be changed?

486. What would the life cycle costs be?

487. How accurate do cost estimates need to be?

488. Vac -variance at completion, how much over/ under budget do you expect to be?

489. What weaknesses do you have?

490. At which frequency ?

491. How will cost estimates be used?

492. Does the suggested change request seem to represent a necessary enhancement to the product?

493. How long are you willing to wait before you find out were late?

494. Is there anything unique in this Situational Leadership projects scope statement that will affect resources?

495. Should a more thorough impact analysis be conducted?

496. Has the documentation relating to operation and maintenance of the product(s) or service(s) been delivered to, and accepted by, operations management?

497. Has operations management formally accepted responsibility for operating and maintaining the product(s) or service(s) delivered by the Situational Leadership project?

498. What can go wrong?

499. How likely is it to go wrong?

500. Definition of done can be traced back to the definitions of what are you providing to the customer in terms of deliverables?

501. Why do you manage cost?

2.24 Quality Management Plan: Situational Leadership

502. Are there nonconformance issues?

503. Who gets results of work?

504. How are changes to procedures made?

505. Who is responsible?

506. What are the appropriate test methods to be used?

507. Are there standards for code development?

508. How are records kept in the office?

509. What data do you gather/use/compile?

510. Was trending evident between reviews?

511. Does the program use modeling in the permitting or decision-making processes?

512. How does your organization use comparative data and information to improve organizational performance?

513. How do you document and correct nonconformances?

514. How do your action plans support the strategic

objectives?

515. How are changes recorded?

516. What are your organizations current levels and trends for the already stated measures related to employee wellbeing, satisfaction, and development?

517. How are data handled when a test is not run per specification?

518. How are your organizations compensation and recognition approaches and the performance management system used to reinforce high performance?

519. What are your results for key measures/indicators of accomplishment of organizational strategy?

520. How will you know that a change is actually an improvement?

521. Does a documented Situational Leadership project organizational policy & plan (i.e. governance model) exist?

2.25 Quality Metrics: Situational Leadership

522. How are requirements conflicts resolved?

523. What is the timeline to meet your goal?

524. Are quality metrics defined?

525. What if the biggest risk to your business were the already stated people who do not complain?

526. Does risk analysis documentation meet standards?

527. What documentation is required?

528. What does this tell us?

529. What percentage are outcome-based?

530. Which report did you use to create the data you are submitting?

531. How do you know if everyone is trying to improve the right things?

532. What metrics do you measure?

533. Who is willing to lead?

534. Have risk areas been identified?

535. What level of statistical confidence do you use?

536. Has risk analysis been adequately reviewed?

537. What group is empowered to define quality requirements?

538. What are your organizations expectations for its quality Situational Leadership project?

539. What metrics are important and most beneficial to measure?

540. What makes a visualization memorable?

541. Is material complete (and does it meet the standards)?

2.26 Process Improvement Plan: Situational Leadership

542. Why quality management?

543. Are you making progress on the improvement framework?

544. The motive is determined by asking, Why do you want to achieve this goal?

545. Are you making progress on the goals?

546. Have the supporting tools been developed or acquired?

547. What personnel are the change agents for your initiative?

548. Are you making progress on your improvement plan?

549. How do you measure?

550. Are you meeting the quality standards?

551. Where do you focus?

552. Does explicit definition of the measures exist?

553. Are there forms and procedures to collect and record the data?

554. What is the return on investment?

555. What personnel are the champions for the initiative?

556. What lessons have you learned so far?

557. Modeling current processes is great, and will you ever see a return on that investment?

558. To elicit goal statements, do you ask a question such as, What do you want to achieve?

559. If a process improvement framework is being used, which elements will help the problems and goals listed?

560. Purpose of goal: the motive is determined by asking, why do you want to achieve this goal?

2.27 Responsibility Assignment Matrix: Situational Leadership

561. Actual cost of work performed?

562. Evaluate the performance of operating organizations?

563. Are all authorized tasks assigned to identified organizational elements?

564. Can the contractor substantiate work package and planning package budgets?

565. Budgeted cost for work scheduled?

566. Most people let you know when others re too busy, and are others really too busy?

567. Incurrence of actual indirect costs in excess of budgets, by element of expense?

568. Is accountability placed at the lowest-possible level within the Situational Leadership project so that decisions can be made at that level?

569. Why cost benefit analysis?

570. The already stated responsible for the establishment of budgets and assignment of resources for overhead performance?

571. Are too many reports done in writing instead of

verbally?

572. Changes in the current direct and Situational Leadership projected base?

573. Who is the Situational Leadership project Manager?

574. What are some important Situational Leadership project communications management tools?

575. How do you manage remotely to staff in other Divisions?

2.28 Roles and Responsibilities: Situational Leadership

576. What should you highlight for improvement?

577. Once the responsibilities are defined for the Situational Leadership project, have the deliverables, roles and responsibilities been clearly communicated to every participant?

578. Does your vision/mission support a culture of quality data?

579. Key conclusions and recommendations: Are conclusions and recommendations relevant and acceptable?

580. What is working well?

581. Are Situational Leadership project team roles and responsibilities identified and documented?

582. What areas would you highlight for changes or improvements?

583. Influence: what areas of organizational decision making are you able to influence when you do not have authority to make the final decision?

584. Who is responsible for each task?

585. What should you do now to ensure that you are exceeding expectations and excelling in your current

position?

586. Was the expectation clearly communicated?

587. What should you do now to prepare for your career 5+ years from now?

588. What should you do now to ensure that you are meeting all expectations of your current position?

589. Does the team have access to and ability to use data analysis tools?

590. How is your work-life balance?

591. Are the quality assurance functions and related roles and responsibilities clearly defined?

592. Are governance roles and responsibilities documented?

593. Implementation of actions: Who are the responsible units?

2.29 Human Resource Management Plan: Situational Leadership

594. Has the budget been baselined?

595. Situational Leadership project Objectives?

596. How will the Situational Leadership project manage expectations & meet needs and requirements?

597. Is there an approved case?

598. How to convince employees that this is a necessary process?

599. Have stakeholder accountabilities & responsibilities been clearly defined?

600. Specific - is the objective clear in terms of what, how, when, and where the situation will be changed?

601. Has the business need been clearly defined?

602. Is a payment system in place with proper reviews and approvals?

603. Is there a Quality Management Plan?

604. How are superior performers differentiated from average performers?

605. Were the budget estimates reasonable?

606. Quality of people required to meet the forecast needs of the department?

607. Are enough systems & user personnel assigned to the Situational Leadership project?

608. Who are the people that make up your organization and whom create the success that your organization enjoys as a whole?

609. Does the schedule include Situational Leadership project management time and change request analysis time?

2.30 Communications Management Plan: Situational Leadership

610. What is Situational Leadership project communications management?

611. How often do you engage with stakeholders?

612. How did the term stakeholder originate?

613. Do you have members of your team responsible for certain stakeholders?

614. What approaches to you feel are the best ones to use?

615. What data is going to be required?

616. What is the stakeholders level of authority?

617. What approaches do you use?

618. Why do you manage communications?

619. Do you feel a register helps?

620. What communications method?

621. What steps can you take for a positive relationship?

622. Is there an important stakeholder who is actively opposed and will not receive messages?

623. Who were proponents/opponents?

624. Who is involved as you identify stakeholders?

625. Are you constantly rushing from meeting to meeting?

626. Which stakeholders can influence others?

627. Who to share with?

2.31 Risk Management Plan: Situational Leadership

628. Internal technical and management reviews?

629. Monitoring -what factors can you track that will enable you to determine if the risk is becoming more or less likely?

630. How quickly does each item need to be resolved?

631. Do you have a mechanism for managing change?

632. Are the participants able to keep up with the workload?

633. Do the people have the right combinations of skills?

634. Have top software and customer managers formally committed to support the Situational Leadership project?

635. How can the process be made more effective or less cumbersome (process improvements)?

636. Does the customer have a solid idea of what is required?

637. Should the risk be taken at all?

638. Are there alternative opinions/solutions/ processes you should explore?

639. Was an original risk assessment/risk management plan completed?

640. Have you worked with the customer in the past?

641. Is the necessary data being captured and is it complete and accurate?

642. Workarounds are determined during which step of risk management?

643. Is security a central objective?

644. Do benefits and chances of success outweigh potential damage if success is not attained?

645. Anticipated volatility of the requirements?

646. Are the required plans included, such as nonstructural flood risk management plans?

2.32 Risk Register: Situational Leadership

647. Are your objectives at risk?

648. What will be done?

649. What is the probability and impact of the risk occurring?

650. What is the appropriate level of risk management for this Situational Leadership project?

651. Which key risks have ineffective responses or outstanding improvement actions?

652. Assume the event happens, what is the Most Likely impact?

653. Contingency actions - planned actions to reduce the immediate seriousness of the risk when it does occur. What should you do when?

654. Why would you develop a risk register?

655. Risk documentation: what reporting formats and processes will be used for risk management activities?

656. When will it happen?

657. What are the main aims, objectives of the policy, strategy, or service and the intended outcomes?

658. What action, if any, has been taken to respond to the risk?

659. What may happen or not go according to plan?

660. Cost/benefit – how much will the proposed mitigations cost and how does this cost compare with the potential cost of the risk event/situation should it occur?

661. People risk -are people with appropriate skills available to help complete the Situational Leadership project?

662. What can be done about it?

663. Having taken action, how did the responses effect change, and where is the Situational Leadership project now?

664. Who needs to know about this?

2.33 Probability and Impact Assessment: Situational Leadership

665. My Situational Leadership project leader has suddenly left your organization, what do you do?

666. Is the customer willing to commit significant time to the requirements gathering process?

667. Are the risk data complete?

668. How risk averse are you?

669. What will be cost of redeployment of personnel?

670. What are the channels available for distribution to the customer?

671. Costs associated with late delivery or a defective product?

672. What is the likelihood?

673. Management -what contingency plans do you have if the risk becomes a reality?

674. What are the chances the risk event will occur?

675. Do requirements demand the use of new analysis, design, or testing methods?

676. Assumptions analysis -what assumptions have you made or been given about your Situational

Leadership project?

677. Can you avoid altogether some things that might go wrong?

678. How much is the probability of a risk occurring?

679. Have staff received necessary training?

680. Who are the international/overseas Situational Leadership project partners (equipment supplier/supplier/consultant/contractor) for this Situational Leadership project?

681. Has something like this been done before?

682. How do you maximize short-term return on investment?

683. Is the technology to be built new to your organization?

2.34 Probability and Impact Matrix: Situational Leadership

684. How are the local factors going to affect the absorption?

685. Which is an input to the risk management process?

686. Does the Situational Leadership project team have experience with the technology to be implemented?

687. What will be cost of redeployment of the personnel?

688. Are tool mentors available?

689. What can you do about it?

690. Will there be an increase in the political conservatism?

691. Which risks need to move on to Perform Quantitative Risk Analysis?

692. How should you structure risks?

693. Degree of confidence in estimated size estimate?

694. Lay ground work for future returns?

695. Are people attending meetings and doing work?

696. Mitigation -how can you avoid the risk?

697. What do you expect?

698. How realistic is the timing of introduction?

699. Can it be enlarged by drawing people from other areas of your organization?

700. Several experts are offsite, and wish to be included. How can this be done?

2.35 Risk Data Sheet: Situational Leadership

701. If it happens, what are the consequences?

702. What are you weak at and therefore need to do better?

703. Whom do you serve (customers)?

704. How can hazards be reduced?

705. What if client refuses?

706. What can you do?

707. What were the Causes that contributed?

708. What do you know?

709. Who has a vested interest in how you perform as your organization (our stakeholders)?

710. What are your core values?

711. Will revised controls lead to tolerable risk levels?

712. What is the likelihood of it happening?

713. What are you here for (Mission)?

714. How do you handle product safely?

715. Has a sensitivity analysis been carried out?

716. What do people affected think about the need for, and practicality of preventive measures?

717. Potential for recurrence?

718. What will be the consequences if the risk happens?

719. What can happen?

2.36 Procurement Management Plan: Situational Leadership

720. Are software metrics formally captured, analyzed and used as a basis for other Situational Leadership project estimates?

721. Is there a formal set of procedures supporting Stakeholder Management?

722. Are vendor invoices audited for accuracy before payment?

723. Pareto diagrams, statistical sampling, flow charting or trend analysis used quality monitoring?

724. Are risk triggers captured?

725. Is there a formal process for updating the Situational Leadership project baseline?

726. Are non-critical path items updated and agreed upon with the teams?

727. Are the results of quality assurance reviews provided to affected groups & individuals?

728. Were Situational Leadership project team members involved in detailed estimating and scheduling?

729. Have Situational Leadership project management standards and procedures been

identified / established and documented?

730. Are the Situational Leadership project team members located locally to the users/stakeholders?

731. Is the Situational Leadership project sponsor clearly communicating the business case or rationale for why this Situational Leadership project is needed?

732. Is the assigned Situational Leadership project manager a PMP (Certified Situational Leadership project manager) and experienced?

733. Does a documented Situational Leadership project organizational policy & plan (i.e. governance model) exist?

734. Are Situational Leadership project team members committed fulltime?

735. Are Situational Leadership project contact logs kept up to date?

736. Has a provision been made to reassess Situational Leadership project risks at various Situational Leadership project stages?

2.37 Source Selection Criteria: Situational Leadership

737. How long will it take for the purchase cost to be the same as the lease cost?

738. What source selection software is your team using?

739. When and what information can be considered with offerors regarding past performance?

740. What can not be disclosed?

741. How will you evaluate offerors proposals?

742. What should clarifications include?

743. How and when do you enter into Situational Leadership project Procurement Management?

744. What is cost analysis and when should it be performed?

745. What benefits are accrued from issuing a DRFP in advance of issuing a final RFP?

746. What are the guidelines regarding award without considerations?

747. What should be considered?

748. Why promote competition?

749. Do you have designated specific forms or worksheets?

750. Does the evaluation of any change include an impact analysis; how will the change affect the scope, time, cost, and quality of the goods or services being provided?

751. How should comments received in response to a RFP be handled?

752. How do you consolidate reviews and analysis of evaluators?

753. How do you encourage efficiency and consistency?

754. When must you conduct a debriefing?

755. Are there any common areas of weaknesses or deficiencies in the proposals in the competitive range?

756. How do you ensure an integrated assessment of proposals?

2.38 Stakeholder Management Plan: Situational Leadership

757. Have all documents been archived in a Situational Leadership project repository for each release?

758. Is there an issues management plan in place?

759. Are formal code reviews conducted?

760. Does the Situational Leadership project have a Quality Culture?

761. Do Situational Leadership project teams & team members report on status / activities / progress?

762. Have key stakeholders been identified?

763. Are metrics used to evaluate and manage Vendors?

764. Has a Situational Leadership project Communications Plan been developed?

765. Where to get additional help?

766. At what point will the Situational Leadership project be closed and what will be done to formally close the Situational Leadership project?

767. Have external dependencies been captured in the schedule?

768. Are all payments made according to the contract(s)?

769. Are the Situational Leadership project team members located locally to the users/stakeholders?

770. Is staff trained on the software technologies that are being used on the Situational Leadership project?

2.39 Change Management Plan: Situational Leadership

771. Has the training provider been established?

772. How do you gain sponsors buy-in to the communication plan?

773. Who might be able to help you the most?

774. Why is the initiative is being undertaken - What are the business drivers?

775. Who will do the training?

776. What are you trying to achieve as a result of communication?

777. Will the readiness criteria be met prior to the training roll out?

778. What is the negative impact of communicating too soon or too late?

779. How far reaching in your organization is the change?

780. Who will fund the training?

781. What goal(s) do you hope to accomplish?

782. How will the stakeholders share information and transfer knowledge?

783. Do you need new systems?

784. Will a different work structure focus people on what is important?

785. Impact of systems implementation on organization change?

786. What are the needs, priorities and special interests of the audience?

787. Readiness -what is a successful end state?

788. What are the major changes to processes?

789. Who will be the change levers?

3.0 Executing Process Group: Situational Leadership

790. What are the main types of goods and services being outsourced?

791. What is the difference between using brainstorming and the Delphi technique for risk identification?

792. What is involved in the solicitation process?

793. It under budget or over budget?

794. What areas were overlooked on this Situational Leadership project?

795. How do you control progress of your Situational Leadership project?

796. Does the Situational Leadership project team have enough people to execute the Situational Leadership project plan?

797. Were sponsors and decision makers available when needed outside regularly scheduled meetings?

798. Does the Situational Leadership project team have the right skills?

799. Are decisions made in a timely manner?

800. What were things that you need to improve?

801. After how many days will the lease cost be the same as the purchase cost for the equipment?

802. How can software assist in procuring goods and services?

803. On which process should team members spend the most time?

804. Will a new application be developed using existing hardware, software, and networks?

805. Do your results resemble a normal distribution?

806. How can you use Microsoft Situational Leadership project and Excel to assist in Situational Leadership project risk management?

807. Just how important is your work to the overall success of the Situational Leadership project?

808. What were things that you did very well and want to do the same again on the next Situational Leadership project?

3.1 Team Member Status Report: Situational Leadership

809. Is there evidence that staff is taking a more professional approach toward management of your organizations Situational Leadership projects?

810. Are the products of your organizations Situational Leadership projects meeting customers objectives?

811. How it is to be done?

812. What is to be done?

813. How does this product, good, or service meet the needs of the Situational Leadership project and your organization as a whole?

814. When a teams productivity and success depend on collaboration and the efficient flow of information, what generally fails them?

815. What specific interest groups do you have in place?

816. How will resource planning be done?

817. How can you make it practical?

818. Will the staff do training or is that done by a third party?

819. Do you have an Enterprise Situational Leadership project Management Office (EPMO)?

820. Does your organization have the means (staff, money, contract, etc.) to produce or to acquire the product, good, or service?

821. Does the product, good, or service already exist within your organization?

822. Are the attitudes of staff regarding Situational Leadership project work improving?

823. How much risk is involved?

824. Are your organizations Situational Leadership projects more successful over time?

825. The problem with Reward & Recognition Programs is that the truly deserving people all too often get left out. How can you make it practical?

826. Does every department have to have a Situational Leadership project Manager on staff?

827. Why is it to be done?

3.2 Change Request: Situational Leadership

828. What is the relationship between requirements attributes and attributes like complexity and size?

829. How well do experienced software developers predict software change?

830. What is the relationship between requirements attributes and reliability?

831. What are the duties of the change control team?

832. What kind of information about the change request needs to be captured?

833. Why control change across the life cycle?

834. Are you implementing itil processes?

835. What has an inspector to inspect and to check?

836. Has your address changed?

837. How is quality being addressed on the Situational Leadership project?

838. How fast will change requests be approved?

839. Where do changes come from?

840. Why do you want to have a change control

system?

841. Which requirements attributes affect the risk to reliability the most?

842. Are there requirements attributes that can discriminate between high and low reliability?

843. What are the requirements for urgent changes?

844. Will all change requests and current status be logged?

845. How shall the implementation of changes be recorded?

846. How does your organization control changes before and after software is released to a customer?

847. What is the purpose of change control?

3.3 Change Log: Situational Leadership

848. How does this change affect the timeline of the schedule?

849. Is the change request open, closed or pending?

850. When was the request submitted?

851. Is this a mandatory replacement?

852. How does this change affect scope?

853. Is the requested change request a result of changes in other Situational Leadership project(s)?

854. When was the request approved?

855. How does this relate to the standards developed for specific business processes?

856. Who initiated the change request?

857. Is the change request within Situational Leadership project scope?

858. Is the change backward compatible without limitations?

859. Do the described changes impact on the integrity or security of the system?

860. Is the submitted change a new change or a modification of a previously approved change?

861. Does the suggested change request represent a desired enhancement to the products functionality?

862. Will the Situational Leadership project fail if the change request is not executed?

3.4 Decision Log: Situational Leadership

863. Do strategies and tactics aimed at less than full control reduce the costs of management or simply shift the cost burden?

864. What are the cost implications?

865. How do you know when you are achieving it?

866. How effective is maintaining the log at facilitating organizational learning?

867. Is your opponent open to a non-traditional workflow, or will it likely challenge anything you do?

868. Adversarial environment. is your opponent open to a non-traditional workflow, or will it likely challenge anything you do?

869. Does anything need to be adjusted?

870. Who will be given a copy of this document and where will it be kept?

871. Meeting purpose; why does this team meet?

872. Which variables make a critical difference?

873. What is the line where eDiscovery ends and document review begins?

874. How does provision of information, both in terms of content and presentation, influence acceptance of alternative strategies?

875. Behaviors; what are guidelines that the team has identified that will assist them with getting the most out of team meetings?

876. Decision-making process; how will the team make decisions?

877. How consolidated and comprehensive a story can you tell by capturing currently available incident data in a central location and through a log of key decisions during an incident?

878. What eDiscovery problem or issue did your organization set out to fix or make better?

879. Is everything working as expected?

880. Who is the decisionmaker?

881. What alternatives/risks were considered?

882. Linked to original objective?

3.5 Quality Audit: Situational Leadership

883. What review processes are in place for your organizations major activities?

884. What are you trying to accomplish with this audit?

885. How does your organization know that its range of activities are being reviewed as rigorously and constructively as they could be?

886. How does your organization know that its systems for assisting staff with career planning and employment placements are appropriately effective and constructive?

887. Are the intentions consistent with external obligations (such as applicable laws)?

888. How does your organization know that its system for attending to the health and wellbeing of its staff is appropriately effective and constructive?

889. What mechanisms exist for identification of staff development needs?

890. How does your organization know that it is effectively and constructively guiding staff through to timely completion of tasks?

891. For each device to be reconditioned, are device

specifications, such as appropriate engineering drawings, component specifications and software specifications, maintained?

892. How does your organization know that its system for ensuring that its training activities are appropriately resourced and support is appropriately effective and constructive?

893. Do the suppliers use a formal quality system?

894. How do you know what, specifically, is required of you in your work?

895. How does your organization know that its system for examining work done is appropriately effective and constructive?

896. How does your organization know that its advisory services are appropriately effective and constructive?

897. What experience do staff have in the type of work that the audit entails?

898. How does your organization know that its research funding systems are appropriately effective and constructive in enabling quality research outcomes?

899. How does your organization know that its Mission, Vision and Values Statements are appropriate and effectively guiding your organization?

900. How does your organization know that the range and quality of its accommodation, catering and

transportation services are appropriately effective and constructive?

901. Has a written procedure been established to identify devices during all stages of receipt, reconditioning, distribution and installation so that mix-ups are prevented?

902. Do the acceptance procedures and specifications include the criteria for acceptance/rejection, define the process to be used, and specify the measuring and test equipment that is to be used?

3.6 Team Directory: Situational Leadership

903. Who should receive information (all stakeholders)?

904. Have you decided when to celebrate the Situational Leadership projects completion date?

905. Who are the Team Members?

906. Who is the Sponsor?

907. Days from the time the issue is identified?

908. What are you going to deliver or accomplish?

909. Why is the work necessary?

910. Who will talk to the customer?

911. When does information need to be distributed?

912. Process decisions: are contractors adequately prosecuting the work?

913. Who will be the stakeholders on your next Situational Leadership project?

914. How and in what format should information be presented?

915. Process decisions: how well was task order work

performed?

916. Contract requirements complied with?

917. How will you accomplish and manage the objectives?

918. Process decisions: is work progressing on schedule and per contract requirements?

919. Timing: when do the effects of communication take place?

920. Does a Situational Leadership project team directory list all resources assigned to the Situational Leadership project?

3.7 Team Operating Agreement: Situational Leadership

921. Do team members need to frequently communicate as a full group to make timely decisions?

922. Do you call or email participants to ensure understanding, follow-through and commitment to the meeting outcomes?

923. Do you ensure that all participants know how to use the required technology?

924. How will you resolve conflict efficiently and respectfully?

925. What are some potential sources of conflict among team members?

926. What are the boundaries (organizational or geographic) within which you operate?

927. Do you begin with a question to engage everyone?

928. Are there more than two functional areas represented by your team?

929. Do you ask participants to close laptops and place mobile devices on silent on the table while the meeting is in progress?

930. Are leadership responsibilities shared among team members (versus a single leader)?

931. What administrative supports will be put in place to support the team and the teams supervisor?

932. Are team roles clearly defined and accepted?

933. Must your team members rely on the expertise of other members to complete tasks?

934. Have you set the goals and objectives of the team?

935. Do you send out the agenda and meeting materials in advance?

936. What is teaming?

937. How will you divide work equitably?

938. Why does your organization want to participate in teaming?

939. Are there more than two native languages represented by your team?

940. How does teaming fit in with overall organizational goals and meet organizational needs?

3.8 Team Performance Assessment: Situational Leadership

941. What makes opportunities more or less obvious?

942. Do friends perform better than acquaintances?

943. Does more radicalness mean more perceived benefits?

944. Where to from here?

945. What is method variance?

946. How much interpersonal friction is there in your team?

947. To what degree are fresh input and perspectives systematically caught and added (for example, through information and analysis, new members, and senior sponsors)?

948. How do you recognize and praise members for contributions?

949. Delaying market entry: how long is too long?

950. To what degree do team members feel that the purpose of the team is important, if not exciting?

951. To what degree can the team ensure that all members are individually and jointly accountable for the teams purpose, goals, approach, and work-

products?

952. To what degree does the teams work approach provide opportunity for members to engage in results-based evaluation?

953. What are teams?

954. To what degree can all members engage in open and interactive considerations?

955. To what degree are the goals ambitious?

956. To what degree do team members agree with the goals, relative importance, and the ways in which achievement will be measured?

957. To what degree do all members feel responsible for all agreed-upon measures?

958. What do you think is the most constructive thing that could be done now to resolve considerations and disputes about method variance?

959. How does Situational Leadership project termination impact Situational Leadership project team members?

960. Do you promptly inform members about major developments that may affect them?

3.9 Team Member Performance Assessment: Situational Leadership

961. To what degree do team members articulate the teams work approach?

962. How do you implement Cost Reduction?

963. Has the appropriate access to relevant data and analysis capability been granted?

964. What specific plans do you have for developing effective cross-platform assessments in a blended learning environment?

965. What evaluation results did you have?

966. Is it critical or vital to the job?

967. How is the timing of assessments organized (e.g., pre/post-test, single point during training, multiple reassessment during training)?

968. Does adaptive training work?

969. What are the staffs preferences for training on technology-based platforms?

970. What tools are available to determine whether all contract functional and compliance areas of performance objectives, measures, and incentives have been met?

971. How do you start collaborating?

972. To what degree can team members meet frequently enough to accomplish the teams ends?

973. Where can team members go for more detailed information on performance measurement and assessment?

974. Does the rater (supervisor) have to wait for the interim or final performance assessment review to tell an employee that the employees performance is unsatisfactory?

975. In what areas would you like to concentrate your knowledge and resources?

976. What resources do you need?

977. How was the determination made for which training platforms would be used (i.e., media selection)?

978. What evaluation results do you have?

3.10 Issue Log: Situational Leadership

979. Who reported the issue?

980. Are they needed?

981. Who is the stakeholder?

982. What would have to change?

983. In classifying stakeholders, which approach to do so are you using?

984. In your work, how much time is spent on stakeholder identification?

985. Is access to the Issue Log controlled?

986. What steps can you take for positive relationships?

987. Are there common objectives between the team and the stakeholder?

988. What is a Stakeholder?

989. Who needs to know and how much?

990. Why not more evaluators?

991. Are there too many who have an interest in some aspect of your work?

992. What does the stakeholder need from the team?

4.0 Monitoring and Controlling Process Group: Situational Leadership

993. What resources (both financial and non-financial) are available/needed?

994. How many more potential communications channels were introduced by the discovery of the new stakeholders?

995. What were things that you did very well and want to do the same again on the next Situational Leadership project?

996. Mitigate. what will you do to minimize the impact should a risk event occur?

997. How well defined and documented were the Situational Leadership project management processes you chose to use?

998. How do you monitor progress?

999. How were collaborations developed, and how are they sustained?

1000. What kinds of things in particular are you looking for data on?

1001. Where is the Risk in the Situational Leadership project?

1002. What are the goals of the program?

1003. Feasibility: how much money, time, and effort can you put into this?

1004. Are the services being delivered?

1005. Is there adequate validation on required fields?

1006. How is Agile Situational Leadership project Management done?

1007. What do they need to know about the Situational Leadership project?

1008. What good practices or successful experiences or transferable examples have been identified?

1009. Are the necessary foundations in place to ensure the sustainability of the results of the programme?

1010. Change, where should you look for problems?

4.1 Project Performance Report: Situational Leadership

1011. To what degree are the teams goals and objectives clear, simple, and measurable?

1012. To what degree do members articulate the goals beyond the team membership?

1013. To what degree do the structures of the formal organization motivate taskrelevant behavior and facilitate task completion?

1014. To what degree does the team possess adequate membership to achieve its ends?

1015. To what degree will the team ensure that all members equitably share the work essential to the success of the team?

1016. To what degree do team members frequently explore the teams purpose and its implications?

1017. To what degree can team members frequently and easily communicate with one another?

1018. To what degree do team members understand one anothers roles and skills?

1019. To what degree are the members clear on what they are individually responsible for and what they are jointly responsible for?

1020. To what degree does the formal organization make use of individual resources and meet individual needs?

1021. To what degree can the team measure progress against specific goals?

1022. To what degree will the team adopt a concrete, clearly understood, and agreed-upon approach that will result in achievement of the teams goals?

1023. To what degree does the information network communicate information relevant to the task?

1024. To what degree will team members, individually and collectively, commit time to help themselves and others learn and develop skills?

1025. To what degree will the approach capitalize on and enhance the skills of all team members in a manner that takes into consideration other demands on members of the team?

4.2 Variance Analysis: Situational Leadership

1026. Wbs elements contractually specified for reporting of status to your organization (lowest level only)?

1027. Are your organizations and items of cost assigned to each pool identified?

1028. Why are standard cost systems used?

1029. What causes selling price variance?

1030. What costs are avoidable if one or more customers are dropped?

1031. How does the use of a single conversion element (rather than the traditional labor and overhead elements) affect standard costing?

1032. What business event caused the fluctuation?

1033. Budget versus actual. how does the monthly budget compare to actual experience?

1034. Do you identify potential or actual budget-based and time-based schedule variances?

1035. Are overhead costs budgets established on a basis consistent with the anticipated direct business base?

1036. Is budgeted cost for work performed calculated in a manner consistent with the way work is planned?

1037. Who are responsible for the establishment of budgets and assignment of resources for overhead performance?

1038. Is data disseminated to the contractors management timely, accurate, and usable?

1039. What is the expected future profitability of each customer?

1040. Are estimates of costs at completion generated in a rational, consistent manner?

1041. Are there changes in the overhead pool and/or organization structures?

1042. Favorable or unfavorable variance?

1043. Who are responsible for overhead performance control of related costs?

1044. Do the rates and prices remain constant throughout the year?

4.3 Earned Value Status: Situational Leadership

1045. When is it going to finish?

1046. Are you hitting your Situational Leadership projects targets?

1047. Verification is a process of ensuring that the developed system satisfies the stakeholders agreements and specifications; Are you building the product right? What do you verify?

1048. How much is it going to cost by the finish?

1049. If earned value management (EVM) is so good in determining the true status of a Situational Leadership project and Situational Leadership project its completion, why is it that hardly any one uses it in information systems related Situational Leadership projects?

1050. How does this compare with other Situational Leadership projects?

1051. Earned value can be used in almost any Situational Leadership project situation and in almost any Situational Leadership project environment. it may be used on large Situational Leadership projects, medium sized Situational Leadership projects, tiny Situational Leadership projects (in cut-down form), complex and simple Situational Leadership projects and in any market sector. some people, of course, know all about earned value, they have used it for years - but perhaps not as effectively as they could have?

1052. Where are your problem areas?

1053. Where is evidence-based earned value in your organization reported?

1054. What is the unit of forecast value?

1055. Validation is a process of ensuring that the developed system will actually achieve the stakeholders desired outcomes; Are you building the right product? What do you validate?

4.4 Risk Audit: Situational Leadership

1056. Are audit program plans risk-adjusted?

1057. Do your financial policies and procedures ensure that each step in financial handling (receipt, recording, banking, reporting) is not completed by one person?

1058. Tradeoff: how much risk can be tolerated and still deliver the products where they need to be?

1059. Does the Situational Leadership project team have experience with the technology to be implemented?

1060. Are end-users enthusiastically committed to the Situational Leadership project and the system/product to be built?

1061. How do you compare to other jurisdictions when managing the risk of ....?

1062. Does the customer understand the process?

1063. Where will the next scandal or adverse media involving your organization come from?

1064. Are all participants informed of safety issues?

1065. Does your organization have a process for meeting its ongoing taxation obligations?

1066. Who is responsible for what?

1067. What expertise does the Board have on quality, outcomes, and errors?

1068. Is your organization willing to commit significant time to the requirements gathering process?

1069. Which assets are important?

1070. Is the number of people on the Situational Leadership project team adequate to do the job?

1071. What are the boundaries of the auditors responsibility for policing management fidelity?

1072. How effective are your risk controls?

1073. Does your organization have a register of insurance policies detailing all current insurance policies?

4.5 Contractor Status Report: Situational Leadership

1074. Who can list a Situational Leadership project as organization experience, your organization or a previous employee of your organization?

1075. What was the overall budget or estimated cost?

1076. What is the average response time for answering a support call?

1077. If applicable; describe your standard schedule for new software version releases. Are new software version releases included in the standard maintenance plan?

1078. Are there contractual transfer concerns?

1079. Describe how often regular updates are made to the proposed solution. Are corresponding regular updates included in the standard maintenance plan?

1080. How long have you been using the services?

1081. What was the final actual cost?

1082. How is risk transferred?

1083. What are the minimum and optimal bandwidth requirements for the proposed solution?

1084. What was the budget or estimated cost for your

organizations services?

1085. How does the proposed individual meet each requirement?

1086. What was the actual budget or estimated cost for your organizations services?

1087. What process manages the contracts?

4.6 Formal Acceptance: Situational Leadership

1088. What is the Acceptance Management Process?

1089. Do you buy-in installation services?

1090. What function(s) does it fill or meet?

1091. What can you do better next time?

1092. How does your team plan to obtain formal acceptance on your Situational Leadership project?

1093. What was done right?

1094. Do you perform formal acceptance or burn-in tests?

1095. Do you buy pre-configured systems or build your own configuration?

1096. Was the sponsor/customer satisfied?

1097. Does it do what Situational Leadership project team said it would?

1098. Have all comments been addressed?

1099. Who would use it?

1100. Did the Situational Leadership project achieve its MOV?

1101. Was the client satisfied with the Situational Leadership project results?

1102. Did the Situational Leadership project manager and team act in a professional and ethical manner?

1103. Was the Situational Leadership project managed well?

1104. Who supplies data?

1105. General estimate of the costs and times to complete the Situational Leadership project?

1106. Does it do what client said it would?

1107. What lessons were learned about your Situational Leadership project management methodology?

5.0 Closing Process Group: Situational Leadership

1108. What were the desired outcomes?

1109. What were things that you did very well and want to do the same again on the next Situational Leadership project?

1110. What communication items need improvement?

1111. Did the Situational Leadership project team have the right skills?

1112. How will you do it?

1113. If action is called for, what form should it take?

1114. Did the delivered product meet the specified requirements and goals of the Situational Leadership project?

1115. Based on your Situational Leadership project communication management plan, what worked well?

1116. Is this a follow-on to a previous Situational Leadership project?

1117. Will the Situational Leadership project deliverable(s) replace a current asset or group of assets?

1118. What level of risk does the proposed budget represent to the Situational Leadership project?

1119. Were the outcomes different from the already stated planned?

1120. Is the Situational Leadership project funded?

1121. What is the Situational Leadership project Management Process?

1122. What were things that you did well, and could improve, and how?

5.1 Procurement Audit: Situational Leadership

1123. Has it been determined which shared services the procurement function/unit should be part of?

1124. Did the conditions of contract comply with the detail provided in the procurement documents and with the outcome of the procurement procedure followed?

1125. Has the expected benefits from realisation of the procurement Situational Leadership project been calculated?

1126. Where funding is being arranged by borrowings, do corresponding have the necessary approval and legal authority?

1127. Are reports based on sound data available to the already stated responsible for monitoring the performance of contracts?

1128. Is the weighting set coherent, convincing and leaving little scope for arbitrary and random evaluation and ranking?

1129. Were technical requirements set strict enough to guarantee the desired performance without being unnecessarily tight to exclude favourable bids that do not comply with all requirements?

1130. Is there a procedure to summarize bids and

select a vendor?

1131. Are goods generally ordered and received in time to be used in the programs for which they were ordered?

1132. Are approval limits covered in written procedures?

1133. Are the journals and ledgers kept current for all funds?

1134. Do procurement staff, supplier and end user communicate properly?

1135. Is there no evidence of false certifications?

1136. Is a cost/benefit analysis, a cost/effectiveness or a financial analysis considering life-cycle costs performed and is the funding of the procurement guaranteed?

1137. Are requisitions and other purchase requests batched to reduce the number of orders issued?

1138. Were any additional works or deliveries admissible, without recourse to a new procurement procedure?

1139. Is the purchase order form clear and complete so that the vendor understands all terms and conditions?

1140. Access to data, including standing data, and the identification of restriction levels and authorised personnel was in place?

1141. Was suitability of candidates accurately assessed?

1142. Are copies of policies made available to staff members involved in budget preparation and administration?

5.2 Contract Close-Out: Situational Leadership

1143. Was the contract type appropriate?

1144. How is the contracting office notified of the automatic contract close-out?

1145. Have all contract records been included in the Situational Leadership project archives?

1146. Was the contract sufficiently clear so as not to result in numerous disputes and misunderstandings?

1147. Change in attitude or behavior?

1148. Have all contracts been completed?

1149. Change in circumstances?

1150. Has each contract been audited to verify acceptance and delivery?

1151. What is capture management?

1152. How does it work?

1153. What happens to the recipient of services?

1154. How/when used ?

1155. Parties: who is involved?

1156. Have all contracts been closed?

1157. Are the signers the authorized officials?

1158. Was the contract complete without requiring numerous changes and revisions?

1159. Parties: Authorized?

1160. Why Outsource?

1161. Have all acceptance criteria been met prior to final payment to contractors?

1162. Change in knowledge?

5.3 Project or Phase Close-Out: Situational Leadership

1163. Complete yes or no?

1164. What went well?

1165. Which changes might a stakeholder be required to make as a result of the Situational Leadership project?

1166. In addition to assessing whether the Situational Leadership project was successful, it is equally critical to analyze why it was or was not fully successful. Are you including this?

1167. Planned completion date?

1168. Were cost budgets met?

1169. What information did each stakeholder need to contribute to the Situational Leadership projects success?

1170. What can you do better next time, and what specific actions can you take to improve?

1171. What information is each stakeholder group interested in?

1172. Did the delivered product meet the specified requirements and goals of the Situational Leadership project?

1173. If you were the Situational Leadership project sponsor, how would you determine which Situational Leadership project team(s) and/or individuals deserve recognition?

1174. What was the preferred delivery mechanism?

1175. What process was planned for managing issues/ risks?

1176. When and how were information needs best met?

1177. Is there a clear cause and effect between the activity and the lesson learned?

1178. Who controlled the resources for the Situational Leadership project?

1179. What is in it for you?

1180. Was the schedule met?

5.4 Lessons Learned: Situational Leadership

1181. What things surprised you on the Situational Leadership project that were not in the plan?

1182. What is in the future?

1183. How mature are the observations?

1184. How efficient were Situational Leadership project team meetings conducted?

1185. How well does the product or service the Situational Leadership project produced meet your needs?

1186. How was the political and social history changed over the life of the Situational Leadership project?

1187. How useful do individuals find communications?

1188. What on the Situational Leadership project worked well and was effective in the delivery of the product?

1189. What are your lessons learned that you will keep in mind for the next Situational Leadership project you participate in?

1190. What are the conceptual limits of the research?

1191. What are the Benefits of Measurements?

1192. How effective was each Situational Leadership project Team member in fulfilling his/her role?

1193. How well is the build process working?

1194. How efficient is the deliverable?

1195. How adequately involved did you feel in Situational Leadership project decisions?

1196. Overall, how effective was the performance of the Situational Leadership project Manager?

1197. Whom to share Lessons Learned Information with?

1198. How effectively were issues managed on the Situational Leadership project?

1199. Were the aims and objectives achieved?

Index

devices   237, 240
diagram   3, 43, 173-174, 184
diagrams   158, 217
Dictionary   3, 162
differ   94, 129
difference   56, 113, 115, 137, 157, 166, 180, 225, 233
different   7, 18, 21, 23-26, 43-44, 53, 79, 84, 88, 107, 109,
120-123, 132, 149, 159, 224, 262
difficult 79, 88, 99, 105, 109, 128, 167, 169, 173, 177, 180
difficulty   110
diffusion   20
digital 28, 86, 92, 112
diplomatic   79
direct   17, 20, 31, 35, 37, 39-40, 42, 46, 52-53, 61, 63, 71, 78, 80-
81, 83, 85, 87, 90, 95, 102, 104, 106-107, 120, 123, 126-127, 129,
133, 162-163, 200, 251
directed   36, 79
directing   61, 80, 88, 94, 133
direction   31-35, 38-40, 43, 47, 52-55, 61, 68-70, 72-74, 77-
82, 84-85, 87-89, 91-92, 95-96, 99-107, 109-110, 113-117, 119-122,
124-128, 130-133, 146
directions   89, 92, 102, 110, 122, 132
directive   98-99, 110, 117
directives   113
directly 1, 21, 34-35, 38, 40-41, 43, 48-49, 54, 63, 86, 112-113, 115-
116, 127-128, 130, 132, 134
director   17-22, 45, 52, 68-69, 72, 80-83, 85-87, 89-90, 97,
99-102, 108, 111-112, 114, 120-121, 124, 127-129, 131
directors   18, 20, 22, 24, 27, 29, 35, 43-44, 47, 49, 51-52, 57,
59, 61, 75, 83, 85, 87, 91, 94-95, 104, 107-108, 112, 114-115, 118-
119, 121, 123-125, 132-133
directory   5, 76, 117, 131, 238-239
directs 111
Disagree   10, 15, 23, 34, 42, 51, 65, 76
disclosed   219
discovered   55
discovery   247
dismissal   123, 129
display 37, 171
displayed   29, 37, 40, 46, 168, 182
disputes   243, 266
diversity   78, 87, 96
divide   241

strength   113, 142
strengthen   93, 107, 123
strengths   172
stress   112
stressful103, 116
stretch 81
strict   263
strong 61, 86, 100, 104, 116
Strongly   10, 15, 23, 34, 42, 51, 65, 76
structure   3-4, 27, 62, 101, 140, 160-161, 177, 213, 224
structured   128
structures   249, 252
styles   18, 79-80, 94, 114, 134
subject8-9, 31
submitted   231-232
submitting   195
succeed   90
succeeded   68, 72
success   17-18, 28, 68, 80, 83, 93, 101, 113, 144, 204, 208,
226-227, 249, 268
successful   53, 60, 66, 72, 97, 117, 137-138, 177-178, 224, 228,
248, 268
succession   75, 118
successor   52
suddenly   211
sufficient   45, 78, 131, 144
suggest   112
suggested   68, 191, 232
suitable   40
summarize   263
superior   132, 203
supervisor   97, 241, 245
supplier   185, 212, 264
suppliers   24, 185, 236
supplies   185, 260
supply 20, 90
support   7, 18, 20-21, 32, 39-40, 43, 46-48, 58, 60, 62-63, 66,
72, 78, 81, 88, 92, 95, 102, 107, 115, 117, 120, 125, 153, 166, 175,
193, 201, 207, 236, 241, 257
supported   33, 46, 98
supporting   21, 50, 57, 60-63, 66, 74, 89, 112, 116, 120, 126,
135, 148, 197, 217
supportive   45, 110

Manufactured by Amazon.ca
Bolton, ON

21007825R00185